Contents

Social and Travel

Work and Study

Appendices

Map of the book

Unit number	Title	Topic	How to ...
Social and Travel			
1	Somewhere to stay	Holiday accommodation	○ write an email in concise, polite, businesslike English, stating your accommodation requirements and asking for further information ○ complete a booking form stating your requirements and asking about the availability of accommodation ○ understand and use a range of accommodation vocabulary and expressions
2	Let's keep in touch	Contacting friends	○ distinguish between letters and emails in terms of style and structure ○ plan and write personal letters and emails ○ write emails using features of informal English typically associated with email writing
3	Forms and more forms	Dealing with bureaucracy	○ understand language commonly used on forms ○ complete forms using appropriate language ○ identify and correct inappropriate language on a form
4	Dear Sir,	Letters to newspapers	○ write a structured letter to a serious newspaper, using formal English ○ use a range of words to qualify your opinions
5	It's not good enough	Letters of complaint about goods and services	○ write a formal letter of complaint ○ avoid repetition when using formal language ○ use a range of expressions appropriate to formal letters of different kinds
Work and Study			
6	This is my life	Writing a CV / résumé	○ write a CV ○ write a covering letter to accompany a CV ○ reduce full sentences to notes
7	Private and confidential	Writing job references	○ recognize the differences between different types of job references ○ write job references in two different formats ○ use relative clauses in formal writing
8	According to our survey	Customer surveys	○ write a report in clear sections and include appropriate sub-headings ○ incorporate reduced relative clauses into your writing
9	The product for you	Taking notes from a product presentation	○ write a note-taking framework ○ take notes from a product presentation ○ reduce complete sentences to noun phrases

Unit number	Title	Topic	How to ...
10	I'll email you	Workplace correspondence	o understand the main differences between traditional letters and emails in work-related contexts o write work-related emails using clear, simple language o incorporate abbreviations and acronyms in emails when appropriate
11	This is the course for me	Writing a personal statement	o write a personal statement in formal, accurate language o express interest and enthusiasm without sounding over-confident o edit and correct inappropriate or incorrect language o write complex sentences incorporating a number of clauses
12	Listen and take note!	Taking notes in a talk or lecture	o listen to a talk or lecture and select key points of information o write notes quickly and economically, omitting words, using symbols, abbreviations and other visual devices o organize notes clearly using numbers, letters and bullets o select key points from written notes
13	Today's seminar	Preparing a classroom presentation	o write prompt cards to refer to during a presentation o write a handout to accompany a presentation o use various devices to highlight key features of a presentation
14	To sum up	Summaries of written texts	o distinguish between key information and unnecessary detail in written texts o write a summary in your own words by paraphrasing original text language o use pronouns and other reference words to ensure that a summary coheres
15	In my view	Arguing a point of view	o plan, structure and write a discursive essay o express ideas and opinions formally in writing o use commas appropriately in formal English
16	According to statistics	Interpreting statistics	o write a structured report based on information presented in tables and graphic form o use a range of expressions to refer to statistical trends and movements

The left side of the table is labelled vertically: **Work and Study**

Acknowledgements

The author would like to thank all the Cambridge University Press team involved in the development of *Real Writing 4* for their commitment, enthusiasm and outstanding support; especially Nóirín Burke, Roslyn Henderson, Caroline Thiriau, Linda Matthews and Martine Walsh. Very special thanks also to Nicholas Murgatroyd for his excellent, sensitive editing. Finally, I would like to thank Val, Laura and Jo for their continuous support.

The author and publishers are grateful to the following reviewers for their valuable insights and suggestions:

Vanessa Boutefeu, Portugal
Ian Chisholm, UK
Helen Cocking, UK
Stephanie Dimond-Bayir, UK
Philip Dover, UK
Rosie Ganne, UK
Jean Greenwood, UK
Sharon Hartle, Italy
Rania Khalil Jabr, Egypt
Hanna Kijowska, Poland
Jessica Mackay, Spain
Marc Sheffner, Japan
Wayne Trotman, Turkey
Tadeusz Z. Wolanski, Poland

The authors and publishers acknowledge the following sources of copyright material and are grateful for the permissions granted. While every effort has been made, it has not always been possible to identify the sources of all the material used, or to trace all copyright holders. If any omissions are brought to our notice, we will be happy to include the appropriate acknowledgements on reprinting.

p. 19: US State Department 'Non Immigrant Visa Application Form'. Copyright © US State Department; p. 27: Howtocomplain.com for the 'Did you know' information taken from the website www.howtocomplain.com. Used by kind permission of howtocomplain.com; p. 45: 'Powerizers product information', p. 92: adapted recording script and audio recording 'Powerizers'. Reproduced by kind permission of Elron Enterprises; p. 52: The University of Manchester Careers Service 'Writing a personal statement – ten tips'. Used by kind permission of The University of Manchester Careers Service; p. 53: Organisation for Economic Co-operation and Development (OECD) 'did you know' statistics, from an OECD Report for the year 2001. Copyright © OECD; p. 57: text 'Speedwriting' from the Wikipedia website en.wikipedia.org/wiki/speedwriting; p. 60: 'word definitions' from *Cambridge Advanced Learner's Dictionary*. Used by permission of Cambridge University Press; p. 65: text 'Mummy DNA Reveals Birth of Ancient Scourge' by David Biello, from www.sciam.com,

News section, 6 October 2006; p. 66: text 'Jurassic "beaver" is largest early mammal yet' by David Biello from www.sciam.com, News Section, 24 February 2006. Copyright © 2006 by Scientific American, Inc. All rights reserved; p. 71: adapted article 'Florida's rangers battle invasion of the giant pythons' by Paul Harris, *The Guardian*, 29 July 2007. Copyright © Guardian News & Media Ltd, 2007; p. 72: 'Unemployment rates by country and year graph' and p. 75: 'United States –Active labour force chart' Copyright © United Nations. United Nations is the author of the original material; p. 72: 'Employment rates in Europe 2005' Copyright © European Communities; p. 73: extract from 'A report on unemployment', p. 73: 'Consumer Durables' graph, p. 80: extract 'Sensory development' from Post Report 140, Early Years Learning, June 2000. Crown Copyright © 2007; p. 80: extract from *The Cambridge Encyclopedia of Language* by David Crystal. Copyright © 1987 David Crystal. Used by permission of Cambridge University Press; p. 81: 'Table of top five languages used on the web' from the website www.internetworldstats.com/stats7.htm; pp. 93–94: adapted recording script and audio recording 'Reasons to be cheerful' by Bob Holmes, Kurt Kleiner, Kate Douglas and Michael Bond. NewScientist, 4 October 2003. Used by permission of NewScientist Magazine.

The publishers are grateful to the following for permission to reproduce copyright photographs and material:

Key: l = left, c = centre, r = right, t = top, b = bottom

Advertising Archives for p. 60; Alamy/©Christophe Testi for p. 11 (r) /©Helene Rogers for p. 11 (c) /©David Pearson for p. 42 /©Westend61 for p. 53 /©Visual Arts Library (London) for p65; Beattie Group for p. 44 (br); Corbis Images/Varie/Alt for p. 23 /©David Turnley for p. 24 /©Douglas Keister for p. 44 (tr) /©Sygma/Julio Donoso for p. 74 /©Charles Cullung/Zefa for p. 80; Getty Images/©Taxi for pp. 11 (l) & 79 (t); La Cafetiere exclusive distributors of Bialetti Products for p. 46 (br); PA Photos/©AP for p. 44 (bl); Photolibrary/©Fancy for p. 75; Punchstock/©Digital Vision for p.33 /©Stockbyte for p. 46 (tl); Rex/©Sipa Press for p. 70; Superstock for p. 79 (b); www.gadgetshop.com for pp. 44 (tl), 47 (l), 47 (r).

Illustrations:

Kathy Baxendale pp. 54, 66; Mark Duffin pp. 10, 17, 63; Kamae Design pp. 72, 73; Katie Mac pp. 36, 74; Julian Mosedale pp. 28, 31, 56

Text design and page make-up: Kamae Design, Oxford
Cover design: Kamae Design, Oxford
Cover photo: © Getty Images
Picture research: Hilary Luckcock

Introduction
To the student

Who is *Real Writing 4* for?

You can use this book if you are a student at advanced level and you want to improve and practise your English writing. You can use the book alone without a teacher or you can use it in a classroom with a teacher.

How will *Real Writing 4* help me with my writing?

Real Writing 4 contains everyday writing tasks. These include writing emails and letters, filling in forms, writing reports and summaries. It is designed to help you with writing you may need to do when communicating with people in English at home or in other countries.

The exercises in each unit help you develop useful skills such as planning, thinking about the reader and checking your work. It is designed to help you with writing you will need to do when communicating in English at home or when visiting another country.

How is *Real Writing 4* organized?

The book has 16 units and is divided into two sections:
- Units 1–5 – social and travel situations
- Units 6–16 – work and study situations

Every unit has:
- *Get ready to write*: to introduce you to the topic of the unit
- *Learning tip*: to help you improve your learning
- *Did you know?*: extra information about vocabulary, different cultures or the topic of the unit.
- *Focus on*: to help you study useful grammar or vocabulary
- *Class bonus*: an exercise you can do with other students or friends
- *Extra practice*: an extra exercise for more practice
- *Can-do checklist*: to help you think about what you learnt in the unit

After each main section, there is a review unit. The reviews help you practise the language and skills you have learnt in each section.

At the back of the book you can find:
- *Appendices*: contain lists of *Useful language* for every unit, useful information about style and register, spelling tips, punctuation and a checklist to use when re-reading a text you have written.
- *Audioscript*: includes everything that you can hear on the audio CD and gives information about the nationalities of the speakers.

- *Answer key*: gives correct answers and possible answers for exercises that have more than one answer. It also gives sample answers for some exercises.

How can I use *Real Writing 4*?

The units in the second section of the book are generally more difficult than the units in the first section. However, you do not need to do the units in a particular order. It is better to choose the units that are most relevant, useful or interesting for you and to do them in the order you prefer.

There are many different ways you can use this book. We suggest you work in this way:
- Identify which areas you want to focus on by using the *Contents* list and find a unit that interests you or go to *Appendix 2*: *Text types* and look for a unit that you might find useful.
- Use the *Get ready to write* section at the start of each unit to help you understand the context.
- Complete the other sections of the unit. At the end of each section check your answers in the *Answer key* or with your teacher.
- Try to do listening exercises without looking at the *Audioscript*. You can read the *Audioscript* after you finish the exercises.
- If your answers are not correct, study the section again to see where you made mistakes.
- When you have completed the *Write* exercise, use the *Check* questions to correct your writing. You can also use *Appendix 6*: *Editing your writing* to check what you have written.
- If you want to do more work on this topic, do the *Extra practice* activity.
- At the end of the unit, think about what you learnt and complete the *Can-do checklist*.
- Go to *Appendix 1* and look at the *Useful language* for the unit again.

Introduction
To the teacher

What is *Cambridge English Skills*?

Real Writing 4 is one of twelve books in the *Cambridge English Skills* series. The series also contains *Real Reading* and *Real Listening & Speaking* books and offers skills training to students from elementary to advanced level. All the books are available in with-answers and without-answers editions.

Level	Book	Author
Elementary CEF: A2 Cambridge ESOL: KET NQF Skills for life: Entry 2	Real Reading 1 with answers	Liz Driscoll
	Real Reading 1 without answers	Liz Driscoll
	Real Writing 1 with answers and audio CD	Graham Palmer
	Real Writing 1 without answers	Graham Palmer
	Real Listening & Speaking 1 with answers and audio CDs (2)	Miles Craven
	Real Listening & Speaking 1 without answers	Miles Craven
Pre-intermediate CEF: B1 Cambridge ESOL: PET NQF Skills for life: Entry 3	Real Reading 2 with answers	Liz Driscoll
	Real Reading 2 without answers	Liz Driscoll
	Real Writing 2 with answers and audio CD	Graham Palmer
	Real Writing 2 without answers	Graham Palmer
	Real Listening & Speaking 2 with answers and audio CDs (2)	Sally Logan & Craig Thaine
	Real Listening & Speaking 2 without answers	Sally Logan & Craig Thaine
Intermediate to upper-intermediate CEF: B2 Cambridge ESOL: FCE NQF Skills for life: Level 1	Real Reading 3 with answers	Liz Driscoll
	Real Reading 3 without answers	Liz Driscoll
	Real Writing 3 with answers and audio CD	Roger Gower
	Real Writing 3 without answers	Roger Gower
	Real Listening & Speaking 3 with answers and audio CDs (2)	Miles Craven
	Real Listening & Speaking 3 without answers	Miles Craven
Advanced CEF: C1 Cambridge ESOL: CAE NQF Skills for life: Level 2	Real Reading 4 with answers	Liz Driscoll
	Real Reading 4 without answers	Liz Driscoll
	Real Writing 4 with answers and audio CD	Simon Haines
	Real Writing 4 without answers	Simon Haines
	Real Listening & Speaking 4 with answers and audio CDs (2)	Miles Craven
	Real Listening & Speaking 4 without answers	Miles Craven

Where are the teacher's notes?

The series is accompanied by a dedicated website containing detailed teaching notes and extension ideas for every unit of every book. Please visit www.cambridge.org/englishskills to access the *Cambridge English Skills* teacher's notes.

What are the main aims of *Real Writing 4*?

- To help students develop writing skills in accordance with the ALTE (Association of Language Testers in Europe) Can-do statements. These statements describe what language users can typically do at different levels and in different contexts. Visit www.alte.org for further information.
- To encourage autonomous learning by focusing on learner training.

What are the key features of *Real Writing 4*?

- It is aimed at advanced learners of English at level C1 of the Council of Europe's CEFR (Common European Framework of Reference for Languages).
- It contains 16 four-page units, divided into two sections: Social and Travel, and Work and Study.
- *Real Writing 4* units contain:
  - *Get ready to write* warm-up exercises to get students thinking about the topic
  - *Focus on* exercises which provide contextualized practice in particular grammar or vocabulary areas
  - *Learning tips* which give students advice on how to improve their writing and their learning
  - *Did you know?* boxes which provide notes on cultural or linguistic differences between English-speaking countries, or factual information on the topic of the unit
  - *Class bonus* communication activities for pairwork and group work so you can adapt the material to suit your class
  - *Extra practice* activities which give students a chance to put into practice the skills learnt
  - *Can-do checklists* at the end of every unit to encourage students to think about what they have learnt
- There are two review units to practise skills that have been introduced in the preceding units.
- It can be used as self-study material, in class, or as supplementary homework material.
- *Real Writing 4* has an international feel and contains a range of native and non-native English accents.

What is the best way to use *Real Writing 4* in the classroom?

The book is designed so that the units may be used in any order, although the more difficult units naturally appear towards the end of the book, in the Work and Study section.

You can consult the unit-by-unit teacher's notes at www.cambridge.org/englishskills for teaching ideas. However, broadly speaking, different parts of the book can be approached in the following ways:

- *Useful language*: You can use the *Useful language* lists in *Appendix 1* to preteach or revise vocabulary and other language from the unit you are working on.
- *Get ready to write*: It is a good idea to use this section as an introduction to the topic. Students can work on these exercises in pairs or groups. Many of these exercises require students to answer questions about their personal experience. These questions can be used as prompts for discussion. Some exercises contain a problem-solving element that students can work on together. Other exercises aim to clarify key vocabulary in the unit. You can present these vocabulary items directly to students.
- *Learning tips*: You can ask students to read and discuss these in an open class situation. An alternative approach is for you to create a series of discussion questions associated with the *Learning tip*. Students can discuss their ideas in pairs or small groups followed by open class feedback. The *Learning tip* acts as a reflective learning tool to help promote learner autonomy.
- *Class bonuses*: The material in these activities aims to provide freer practice. You can set these up carefully, then take the role of observer during the activity so that students carry out the task freely.
- *Extra practice*: These can be set as homework or out-of-class projects for your students. Alternatively, students can do *Extra practice* tasks in pairs during class time
- *Can-do checklists*: Refer to these at the beginning of a lesson to explain to students what the lesson will cover, and again at the end so that students can evaluate their learning for themselves.
- *Appendices*: You may find it useful to refer your students to the *Appendices* for information on style, spelling and punctuation. Students can use *Appendix 6* as a useful checklist for editing their written work.

Unit 1
Somewhere to stay

go to Useful language p. 82

Get ready to write

- Think of one or two adjectives to describe each of these types of accommodation.
- Which types of accommodation have you stayed in?
- What kinds of tourist accommodation are most popular in your country?
- How well are people with disabilities catered for? (Think about people who are blind or use wheelchairs, for example.)
- If you wanted to find out about holiday accommodation, who would you ask and where would you look?

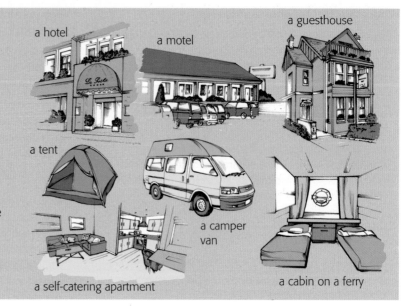

a hotel

a motel

a guesthouse

a tent

a camper van

a self-catering apartment

a cabin on a ferry

Arranging accommodation

Look at examples

1 Look at the email enquiries about holiday accommodation on the opposite page and answer questions a–c.

a What type of accommodation is each group enquiring about?

----

b Who are the people in each group?

----

c What special needs or requirements does each group have?

Did you know …?

The euro was first introduced as an electronic currency in 1999, then, in January 2002, it officially replaced the old national currencies in twelve European Union countries. In order to meet the needs of the twelve countries, more than 15 billion bank notes and 50 billion coins were printed and minted.
Although the pound sterling has not been replaced by the euro, some shops and businesses in Britain accept payment in euros.

2 Read the two examples again. Then answer these questions.

a What do the two enquiries have in common? How are they different? Think about the following:
   - the method of writing and sending
   - the detailed information sent
   - any special requirements mentioned

----

b How are these ways of paying for accommodation different from each other?
credit card / debit card / cheque / bank transfer

----

c The writer of the first enquiry wants *full board*. What other kinds of accommodation do hotels offer?

Group 1

Mountain View Information Request

Hello,

I have just found details of your hotel on the Internet. You seem to offer exactly the kind of facilities I am looking for.

I require accommodation for myself and a group of colleagues for four nights in September next year. These are our details:

• Dates: 2–5 September
• Rooms: four double rooms + two single rooms
• Conference facilities for ten people
• We require full board

I should explain that we are a group of college graduates from Denmark who are in the process of setting up our own company. Our main reason for visiting Australia is to have a relaxing holiday with our partners, but we will also need a room where we can spend time on our business plans. Is there a meeting room in your hotel where we could meet for 2–3 hours each day of our stay? If so, does the room have audio-visual facilities: projector, screen, internet access etc.?

We look forward to hearing from you.

Best wishes,

Nils Andersen

Group 2

Your Comments, Special Needs, etc:

Could you let us know how many rooms and beds there are at the cottage? We need the following: a double room for my partner and me, twin beds for our two boys, a cot for the baby, and a single bed in a downstairs room for my disabled father.

It is also important for us to know whether there is wheelchair access to the cottage from the driveway. My father is completely dependent on his wheelchair.

I have three more questions:
• How far is the cottage from the nearest supermarket or food shops?
• Is the surrounding countryside suitable for walking and cycling?
• Is it possible to pay in euros?

Scottish Cottages

Plan

3 You are going to write an email to a hotel stating your requirements and asking for further information.

a   Read about three hotels and choose the one you would like to stay in for a short break.

The Swan Hotel,
near Oxford, England

The Swan Hotel, situated in a quiet rural area in the southwest of England, has an international reputation for sophisticated elegance. It is ideal for anyone wanting a complete break from their stressful everyday life. Excellent food served in an elegant restaurant; spacious, comfortable lounges and relaxing gardens.

The Central Hotel, Melbourne, Australia

The Central, originally built and opened in 1961, has been completely renovated and upgraded to a 4-star standard. The 86 hotel rooms and suites, restaurant and bar have all been thoroughly refurbished. Recent additions include al fresco eating areas, café, bar and fully-equipped meeting rooms.

Hotel de Paris,
Nice, France

Staying at the Hotel de Paris, in the heart of Nice, you will enjoy our proximity to the town's numerous attractions. Shop, visit the old town, or relax on the beach. And then enjoy the special atmosphere of the hotel and our impeccable service.

b   You are writing the email on behalf of a small group of friends you will be travelling with. One of your group is blind. In preparation for writing, make notes under these headings:
   – the main purpose of your stay: holiday / business? ....
   – length of stay ....
   – number of people (adults / children?) ....
   – type of room(s) required ....
   – special requirements or extra facilities you need ....
   – questions about the area where the hotel is ....
   ....
   – questions about methods of payment ....
   ....

c   Plan your email, paragraph by paragraph, in your notebook. Use the emails on page 11 to help you.
   – Paragraph 1: Say where you found out about the hotel.
   – Paragraph 2: Explain the purpose of your stay if you feel it is necessary, then describe your main requirements concisely, but in detail.
   – Paragraph 3: Enquire about the suitability of the hotel for your blind friend.
   – Paragraph 4: Ask for any further information you would like. Read the hotel description again carefully to find out if you need clarification or more detailed information.

Focus on ...
If so / If not

When you ask a *Yes / No* question in a letter or email, you will sometimes want to ask a follow-up question or make another statement.
You can use:
– *If so,* to mean '*If the answer to my question is yes, …*'
or
– *If not,* to mean '*If the answer to my question is no, …*'

Example:
Is there a meeting room in your hotel where we could meet? **If so,** *does the room have audio-visual facilities?* **If not,** *would it be possible for us to use one of the lounge areas?*

Write *If so,* and *If not,* follow-up questions for these enquiries:
a   Does the hotel cater for special dietary needs?
   ....
   ....
b   Does your hotel have family rooms for parents with young children?
   ....
   ....
c   Do your rooms have internet access?
   ....
   ....

Learning tip

It is not always necessary to make a written plan, but think carefully about the structure of what you are going to write before you start writing. Decide the number and content of paragraphs or sections you are going to write. Remember to start a new paragraph or section for each new topic.

Write

4   In your notebook, write a draft of your email in 150–200 words. Refer to your paragraph plan and the emails on page 11. Your writing should be polite, concise and businesslike.

   – Use full verb forms:
      I have *just found* rather than:
      I've *just found* …
   – Avoid slang or vague language:
      2–3 hours *each day* rather than
      a couple of hours *a day*
      for **ten** *people* rather than for
      about ten *people*
   – Write in short, clear sentences.

Check

5   Read your email carefully, checking these points.

   – Content
      Have you stated your requirements clearly?
      Have you made the special needs of your blind friend clear?
      Have you asked for further information based on the hotel advertisement?
   – Structure
      Is the email organized in clear paragraphs?
   – Style
      Is your writing, polite, concise and businesslike?

6   Write the final version of your email, making any necessary corrections and improvements.

Class bonus

1   Exchange emails with another student, then read and check what they have written. Suggest corrections and other improvements to each other's emails.
2   Imagine you work for the hotel and you receive your partner's email. Write a brief reply.

E X tra practice

Complete the Hotel Registration
Form opposite. Complete the Special
requirements section of the form
in a similar way to the person who
completed the second example on
page 11.

Hotel Registration Form

First Name:

Last Name:

Company/Organization:

Accommodation requirements

Number of double rooms

Number of single rooms

Arrival date   Departure date

Special requirements (Health / Dietary etc.)

Can-do checklist

Tick what you can do.

	Can do	Need more practice
I can write an email in concise, polite, businesslike English, stating my accommodation requirements and asking for further information.		
I can complete a booking form stating my requirements and asking about the availability of accommodation.		
I can understand and use a range of accommodation vocabulary and expressions.		

Unit 2
Let's keep in touch

go to Useful language p. 82

Get ready to write

- Which of these methods do you use to keep in touch with friends? Rank them in order of frequency (1 = most used, 5 = least used).
  - traditional letter sent by post ☐
  - email ☐
  - internet messaging (MSN etc.) ☐
  - telephone (landline or mobile) ☐
  - text message from your mobile ☐

- Which of the above methods would you use:
  - if you needed to contact someone very quickly or urgently? _____
  - if you needed to convey a very personal message, for example to ask for advice or to express sympathy? _____
  - if it had been a long time since you contacted someone? _____
  - if you had no money? _____
  - if you were very short of time? _____

- Think of the three people you contact most frequently. Which methods do you use?

Writing an informal email

Look at examples

1 Look at the three examples of written correspondence on this page and the opposite page.

a Why was each one written?

---

b In what ways are they similar and different?

---

2 Read the three examples again.

a What type of text is each example?

---

b Which is the most formal, and which is the most informal?

c Highlight examples of informal language in texts 1 and 3. Look for the following features:
  - Short verb forms — **I've** been trying
  - Colloquial vocabulary — **hang out** with his **mates**
  - Words left out (ellipsis) — (**It was**) Good to hear from you.
  - Abbreviations — Jon **'n'** Jo

1

⊖ ⊖ ⊖

From:	Matt Greenfield
Sent:	29 October 2007 13:09
To:	Jon Stewart
Subject:	Holidays and stuff

Hi Jon 'n' Jo
Had a great time in Turkey – nice people, nice hotel, good food, perfect weather, interesting trips. Only real prob was flights – both delayed more than 2 hours. Got home last night at 1 o'clock. Glad you had a good time with Pete and Chris and others. Getting together – great idea but Tuesdays aren't good for us – how about Wednesday 21st?
See you soon
Cheers
Matt and Tina
BTW Hope you enjoy Libya.

2

27, Ashley Gardens
Chelwood Gate
West Sussex
RH17 7LF
28th Sept. 2006

Dear Fumiko,

I've just realized that I haven't thanked you for the CD you sent for my birthday. Sorry! I really love The Gotan Project, so much so that I've just started going to a tango dance class that's started in the town. It's amazingly popular.

Things are fine with us. I'm still working part-time at the school, and giving private music lessons, so I don't have much free time. Alex has decided he wants to train to be a radiographer and has just started the long complicated process. He did a preliminary nursing course last year – and he's about to apply for a place on a specialist radiography course. There are usually more applicants than there are places – so it's by no means certain that he'll get accepted. We're all okay. Do you remember my brother Matt, who went to Australia? Well, he's back – this time it looks as though he's here to stay. He was getting fed up with working as a chauffeur and is looking for a different kind of job. Anyway, that's about it for now. Write when you have time. Email me if you'd prefer. I can't believe it's nearly two years since you were here. Do you have any plans to come to Europe again? If so, you must let us know when and where, so that we can meet up.

Thanks again for the present.

Best wishes,
Gemma

3

From:	Silvia
To:	Ed
Subject:	Re: FW: Summer
Date:	Thu, 15 Jun 2006 15:21:14

Hi Marco and Silvia,

I've been trying to email you but the mails keep bouncing back – probably an old email address. I hope this one gets through.

Hi Ed,

Good to hear from you! Sorry about our home email – clever idea to send it to Marco's work address! Marco's really busy, so he's forwarded it to me.

We're writing to tell you that we'll be staying at the campsite near you again this summer. First two weeks of August. This time we're flying, then hiring a car. Hope we can meet again.

Great news! Call us when you're here and we'll arrange a get-together. Perhaps we could go out for a meal – there's several good restaurants near here, like the pizzeria we went to last time. Remember?

Things are really busy here. Jackie's just started working as an assistant in a primary school and I have more freelance photographic work than I can cope with – suppose we shouldn't complain.

Know what you mean. I've just started a new job as a receptionist in a hotel just down the road – very handy, but I have to work weekends and evenings – so no holiday this year and big changes to family life!

Becky's just finished her first exams. In September she'll go to the local college (for 16-18-year-olds). Jo's just coming to the end of her third year at secondary school.

The boys have just started their summer holidays. Gianfranco just scraped through his exams! He'd much rather hang out with his mates. Adriano's done pretty well, but he's got a different attitude to life. Both the boys've got scooters now. They seem to spend all their free time on them. The only good thing is, they're making less phone calls – they didn't used to go out at all.

Anyway, we hope you'll be at home when we're in Italy and that the weather's better than last time we met.

I'm sure we'll be around – just come round or give us a ring.

Best wishes to you all,

Ed and Jackie
Love
Silvia

Plan

3 **You are going to reply by email to a letter from an old friend, saying what you have been doing since you last met a year ago.**

This is part of your friend's letter.

> *Anyway, the real reason I'm writing is to tell you that Sam and I are getting married in June and we'd like you to be at the wedding. We really hope you can make it. When you write back, don't forget to tell us what you've been up to.*
>
> *I can't wait to hear from you – email me if you like.*

Make a list of things to tell your friend. Include some of these areas of your life.

- major changes in your life or circumstances
- family news and news of mutual friends
- education or work

----

4 **Plan your email paragraph by paragraph. Example:**

Paragraph 1	respond to the news in the extract above.
Paragraph 2	changes in your life
Paragraph 3	news about family and friends
Paragraph 4	what has happened to you at school, college or work
Paragraph 5	suggest the two of you keep in touch more regularly

----

Focus on ...
the language of informal emails

- Starting and finishing informal emails:
  Hi (Laura) / Hello (Laura) / Laura (name only)
  *Good to hear from you. / Got the email – thanks /
  See you (then) / Stay in touch / Hope to see you
  soon / Love / Cheers / Speak soon / Take care /
  Best /
  Nick* (name only)
- Acronyms used to save time in emails:
  BTW – by the way / ***IMO*** – in my opinion /
  FYI – for your information
- Short verb forms:
  *we've been having … / we'll arrange … /
  my friends've all got …*
- Colloquial vocabulary:
  loads of (instead of *a lot of*) / *give someone a ring*
  (instead of *phone*) / *glad* (instead of *pleased*) /
  get (instead of *receive*)
- Non-standard grammar (Errors!):
  There's (There are) *twenty students in my class.
  That's **less** (fewer) students than in my last class.
  We didn't **used** (use) to work very hard.*

In your notebook, rewrite these extracts from formal letters using informal language.

1
Dear Matthew

I am writing to thank you for attending our meeting yesterday. In my opinion, it was very useful.
We are sure you will enjoy working with Debbie and John.

I will be in touch again soon.

With best wishes,

Jenny

2
Dear Juan,
Thank you for your letter which we received this morning. We are sorry to hear that you have been made redundant, but very pleased that you are having an interview for another job next Wednesday.
We will be very interested to know whether you are successful. We wish you the best of luck.
Yours sincerely,
Pieter

Learning tip

Anyway at the start of a sentence or paragraph indicates a change of subject. It is especially useful if you want to signal a return to a previous subject, or to show that you are coming to the end of your letter.
It can be used in a similar way in conversation.

Write

5 Imagine that you only have about 15–20 minutes to write your email, so write quickly. Write 200–225 words. Use informal language and end your email by suggesting how the two of you could keep in touch more regularly in the future.

Check

6 Read your email carefully, checking these points.

 – Content Have you responded to the news in your friend's letter?
 Have you managed to include all your own news?
 – Structure Does your email look reader-friendly? Have you broken the information down into easy-to-read chunks?
 – Style Is the language informal?

7 Write the final version of your email, making any necessary corrections and improvements.

Did you know …?

Email is older than the Internet. It started in 1965, and by 1966 it was already possible to send messages between different computers.
The @ sign was introduced into email addresses in 1971 and quickly became standard.

Class bonus

1 Exchange emails with another student and read your partner's email as though you were the person who had written the letter extract on page 16.
2 Write a brief reply, acknowledging the email and responding to the key information and news it contains.

EXtra practice

2 Listen to a message left on your answerphone. Write a brief email reply, responding to the speaker's suggestions.

Can-do checklist

Tick what you can do.

	Can do	Need more practice
I can distinguish between letters and emails in terms of style and structure.		
I can plan and write personal letters and emails.		
I can write emails using features of informal English typically associated with email writing.		

Unit 3
Forms and more forms

go to Useful language p. 82

Get ready to write

- Which of these types of form have you filled in?
  - an application form for an education course or job
  - an insurance application or claim form
  - a passport or visa application form
  - a form applying for a credit card or to open a bank account
  - a tax return form
  - an application to join a club, gym, etc.

- On which of the forms listed in the first exercise would you be likely to find the following?
  a Place of birth / Maiden name _____
  b Approximate value of item being claimed for

     _____
  c Salary for the last financial year _____
  d Briefly describe your injury _____
  e Have you suffered from any of these health problems in the last ten years? _____
  f Do you wish to transfer a balance from another card?

     _____
  g Academic qualifications _____

Completing forms

Look at examples

1 Read these extracts from two completed forms.

a What kind of form do you think each extract is from?

   ....
   ....
   ....

b What other information do you think was required on the forms?

   ....
   ....
   ....

Did you know ...?

In most countries the financial (or *fiscal*) year and the calendar year are the same: 1 January–31 December. For individual taxpayers and some large corporations in Britain, the financial years runs from 1 April–31 March. Historically this was intended to avoid busy periods.

Extract 1

Please complete all questions. If any question is not applicable, please write N/A

Name of Policyholder *Natasha*
Policy No. *79234/HA/73B*

Travel details
Type of travel (Business/Holiday)
holiday to visit family
Please give reason for delay / missed departure
technical problems, but no details provided by airline

Please state **scheduled** times of travel
Date of departure: *03/09/06*
Date of arrival: *Beijing*
Place of departure: *Paris (Charles de Gaulle)*
Place of destination: *04/09/06*
Departure time: *15.55*
Arrival time: *08.55*

Please state **actual** times of travel
Date of departure: *04/09/06*   Departure time: *15.55*
Date of arrival: *05/09/06*   Arrival time: *08.55*

To support your claim, please provide documentary evidence from your tour operator to confirm actual departure and arrival times, and the reason for the delay you encountered.

Extract 2

20. Name and address of present employer or school

Name Central Avenue College   Address Paris

21. Present occupation (If retired, write "retired". If student, write "student".) Student	**22. When do you intend to arrive in the U.S.?** (Provide specific date if known) day month year _____ _____ 2008	**23. Email address** jtc100@yahoo.com

24. At what address will you stay in the U.S.?

Street address line 1

Tassett Court

Street address line 2

_____

City

Santa Cruz

State/Province

California   Barcode

Postal Code

_____

25. Name and telephone numbers of person in U.S. who you will be staying with or visiting for tourism or business

Name Jack Bailey	Home phone Don't know
Business phone Don't know	Cell phone 07986 326715

DO NOT WRITE IN THIS SPACE
|
50mm X 50 mm
|
PHOTO
|
Staple or glue photo here

26. How long do you intend to stay in the US?

Not sure – probably 9–12 months

27. What is the purpose of your trip?

Mainly to improve my English, but I might do a little work

28. Who will pay for your trip? My parents	**29. Have you ever neen in the US?** ○ Yes ○ (No) WHEN? (Most recent) day month year _____ _____ _____ FOR HOW LONG? _____ Enter additional visits to the U.S. here:

2 Read the two extracts again.

a How could the information given be improved? (Look for errors and unclear information.)

Extract 1 _____

_____

_____

_____

_____

Extract 2 _____

_____

_____

_____

_____

b Look at the language in the two extracts. How would you describe the language of the forms themselves? Use appropriate adjectives from the box:

note form	detailed
businesslike	factual
concise	vague
conversational	informal
semi-formal	formal
imprecise	

_____

_____

_____

_____

_____

c How would you describe the language used by the people who have completed the forms?

Extract 1 _____

_____

Extract 2 _____

_____

_____

Focus on ...
language appropriate to forms

1 Read these two extracts from accident report forms and then answer the questions a–c below.

A

State clearly and fully how the accident occurred

I was travelling along South Way at approximately 50kph, when the other car came in from a minor road on the left. As I was on the main road, I thought the driver would stop, but he did not.

B

State clearly and fully how the accident occurred

I was going along South Way about 50kph, when this car came from the left. He should've stopped because I was on the main road, but he didn't – he just kept going.

a Which one is written in a more appropriate style? Why?

b How is the style of the other extract different?

c Where might you expect to read the other?

2 Rewrite this extract from an insurance claim form in appropriate language.

It must've been about 4 o'clock in the afternoon, I suppose. I just nipped out to the bank to get some cash. I was only out of my hotel room for about ten minutes. When I got back, I knew someone had been in. There was stuff all over the floor.

Plan

3 **You are going to complete part of an insurance claim form reporting the loss or theft of some personal possessions while you were on holiday. Prepare for this by noting down the following information, which can be genuine or imaginary.**

– a place you have been to on holiday
– when you went there
– three–four articles you had on this holiday that were valuable or would be difficult to replace. Estimate the value of each article in your own currency.

4 **Look quickly at the extract from the form on the opposite page, but do not start completing it yet. Does it ask you for any information that you would find difficult or impossible to provide?**

Write

5 **Complete the extract from the claim form in as much detail as possible with the information you noted in Exercise 3. Read each question carefully and only give the information required. Write in an appropriate style.**

Learning tip

When you are completing forms, it is advisable to give clear, accurate information wherever possible. Avoid using 'vague' language such as:

probably £50 / **around** 8 January / 8 January – I'm **almost sure** / I **think** it was Thailand

Check

6 **Read through the completed sections of the form carefully, checking these points.**

– Have you given the kind of information that was required?
– Have you answered the questions in full?
– Have you left any sections incomplete?
– Is your handwriting clear and easy to read?

7 **Make any necessary corrections and improvements.**

Class bonus

1 Exchange completed forms with another student and read the information they have written on the form.
2 Take turns to ask each other for more detailed information about the lost or stolen articles. (If you are the questioner, imagine you are an insurance company employee who suspects that this may be a dishonest claim.)

E X tra practice

Which? is an independent organization based in the UK which exists to give consumers advice. Go to their website at www.which.co.uk and follow the links to Travel. See what advice you can find on travel insurance.

Personal Effects Claim Form

Section 2

Travel details
Type of travel: Business / Personal
Please give date of loss / theft _____   In which country did the loss / theft occur? _____
Please give full details of loss / theft
To whom was the loss / theft reported? _____   When was the loss / theft reported? _____
What steps were taken to recover the articles? (Please attach any written evidence.)
Have you had any previous claims on this type of insurance?   YES / NO   If YES, please give details, including dates.

Section 3

Particulars of claim				
Full description of each item of property lost or stolen.	Date of purchase	Original price	Amount claimed	Receipts / replacement estimates attached

Section 4

DECLARATION
I declare that all the information given is to the best of my knowledge and belief, full, true and correct.   Signed _____ Date: _____

Can-do checklist

Tick what you can do.

	Can do	Need more practice
I can understand language commonly used on forms.		
I can complete forms using appropriate language.		
I can identify and correct inappropriate language on a form.		

Unit 4
Dear Sir,

Get ready to write

- Look at the text types in the table and tick ✓ those you have written.

A	B
a letter/email to a newspaper or magazine	a letter giving advice to a friend
a letter/email to a radio or TV station saying what you think about a programme	a holiday postcard to a relative
	an email to a work colleague
a message to an internet forum / message board expressing an opinion	a reply to a friend's party invitation
a factual article for a newsletter	a note to congratulate, thank or apologize to an acquaintance
a report related to your work	

- What is the main difference between the kinds of writing in lists A and B above?
  Think about the following:
  - the person or people who will read each type of writing
  - the style of writing that is normally found in each type of writing – what level of formality would readers expect?
  - the time needed to produce each type of writing

go to Useful language p. 82

A letter to a newspaper

Look at examples

1 **Read the letters to a newspaper on the opposite page and answer these questions.**

   a What is the subject of both letters?

   ----

   b What do the writers think about this subject?

Did you know ...?

Most British daily newspapers have a 'Letters to the editor' section, in which readers give their opinions on news stories, or react to something they have read in the newspaper. Readers' letters or emails are classed as part of the 'Comment' section of a newspaper, which includes leaders and editorial articles.

2 **Letters to serious newspapers tend to be written in quite formal language. Read the letters again and <u>underline</u> examples of a–e.**

   a uncontracted auxiliary verbs
   b polite phrases
   c impersonal style
   d long, complex sentences
   e formal vocabulary and grammar

3 **Make a list of the language the letter writers use to express their ideas and opinions.**
   Example: I think that ...

1

In his letter to your newspaper (25 March), James Green supports the introduction of compulsory ID cards on the grounds that they will put an end to identity theft, help combat organized crime, and reduce the threat from international terrorism. I think that Mr Green is mistaken, as his naive assumptions take no account of the ingenuity of the criminal mind.

My strong personal belief is that the only people who will benefit from ID cards will be professional criminals. Far from putting an end to identity theft, ID cards will provide organized criminals, especially forgers, with a strong financial incentive to produce and sell fake cards to the con men, hackers and would-be terrorists whom Mr Green fears. I genuinely believe that the ordinary citizens of this country will actually be less safe than they are currently.

In addition to this, it is estimated that the cost of the card system will be six billion pounds of taxpayers' money. I am quite sure that, like me, many of your readers can think of better things that such a sum of money could be spent on.

And perhaps most worrying of all is this question: 'Who will have access to the data bank on which my personal details will be stored?' In my view, the government and their agencies already know more about me than is healthy in a democratic society.

When Mr Green has a final demand from his bank to repay a £100,000 loan, his claim that he knows nothing about it will be almost certainly be met with: 'It must have been you who borrowed the money – your ID card was used.'

David Sullivan (by email)

2

As a German citizen, I have carried an ID card with me since the age of 16. It fits into my pocket and has my address on it. The card enables me to open a bank account or to prove that I am the owner of my credit card. In addition, I can travel around Europe without a passport. It seems to me that carrying my ID card actually increases my freedom rather than restricts it.

By contrast, in Britain, people are required to provide household bills – for electricity, or water – to prove who they are and where they live. When I tried to rent a room in London, it was almost impossible, as I did not have any household bills in my name. It also meant that I could not open a bank account or even rent a video.

In my opinion, only criminals and terrorists need to fear the introduction of ID cards. From my own experience, I would say that they make life easier.

Yours faithfully,

Hanna Schwarz

Focus on ...
qualifying opinion expressions

1 Which words from this box could replace the <u>underlined</u> words in phrases a–e? Some words can be used more than once. Remember to choose the appropriate type of word: adjective or adverb.

absolutely	certain	firm	firmly	general
genuine	honest	honestly	official	passionate
passionately	personal	popular	professional	really
seriously	sincere	sincerely	fashionable	pretty
profound	traditional			

a My <u>strong</u> personal belief ...   firm
b I <u>genuinely</u> believe that ...   _____
c I am <u>quite sure</u> that ...   _____
d It's my <u>considered</u> opinion that ...   _____
e The <u>accepted</u> view on this is ...   _____

2 We can also introduce sentences with adverbs to indicate how we think or feel. What other words could replace the underlined adverbs in these sentences?

a <u>Astonishingly</u>, no one was hurt in the accident.
_____

b <u>Obviously</u>, we weren't meant to overhear what they were saying.
_____

c <u>Interestingly</u>, there has been less traffic in the city since road-pricing was introduced.
_____

Plan

4 You are going to write a letter or email expressing your own opinions in reply to this letter written to a newspaper.

a As you read the letter, decide whether you basically agree or disagree with the opinions expressed.

In these days of equality between the sexes, it seems to me perfectly reasonable that, in wartime, women soldiers should be expected to fight alongside their male counterparts on the front line. Unlike your reporter (Ref Why we should continue to protect our women, *The Evening Times*, Friday 13 April) I firmly believe that, given the right training and experience, women are as physically and mentally tough as men.

In my view, those who claim that women are not capable of fighting effectively because of their emotional make-up are guilty of simple, old-fashioned sexism.

Jenny Lavender (Manchester)

b In your notebook, make a list of points to include in your email or letter.
– If you agree with the writer, think of two additional points to support her argument.
– If you disagree, think of two arguments expressing the opposite point of view.
c Plan your writing paragraph by paragraph. Example:
Paragraph 1   State your basic position on the subject, referring to the original letter. Include reference to any relevant experience you have had. (Different approaches are used by writers of the two sample letters on page 23.)
Paragraph 2   Present your first argument.
Paragraph 3   Present your second argument.
Paragraph 4   End with a summary of your views or an additional thought in support of your point of view.

Write

5 Write your first draft letter in 250–300 words. Remember the following points.

– The style of your writing should be formal. (Refer to the list in Exercise 2.)
– Use a variety of phrases to express your ideas and opinions. (Refer to the list you made in Exercise 3.)
– Link ideas within and between paragraphs.

Learning tip

Whatever you are writing, avoid repeating words or phrases, either by using synonyms or alternative constructions. Examples:
– Synonyms:
  *It's my **opinion** that …* / *It's my **belief** that …*
– Alternative constructions:
  ***I think** that …* / ***In my opinion** …*

Check

6 Read your letter carefully, checking these points.

– Content   Have you referred to the original letter?
            Have you expressed your opinions clearly?
– Structure Is the letter organized in clear paragraphs?
            Does each paragraph include one main point?
– Style   Is your writing sufficiently formal?

7 Write the final version of your letter, making any necessary corrections and improvements.

Class bonus

1 Exchange letters with another student, then read carefully what they have written.
2 Write a brief reply to your partner's letter, making it clear whether you agree or disagree with their point of view.

E X tra practice 1

Look at these headlines from a British newspaper. Choose the headline you feel most strongly about and write a letter to the newspaper expressing your feelings.

Congestion charges will ease traffic chaos

Footballer's transfer fee sets new record

Government spending on arms doubles as environmental funding is cut

Family to live on Mars

E X tra practice 2

Scan a current newspaper – it can be in English or your language – to find an article or a story that you have strong feelings about. Choose the story you feel most strongly about and write a short letter to a newspaper expressing your opinions.

Can-do checklist

Tick what you can do.

	Can do	Need more practice
I can write a structured letter to a serious newspaper, using formal English.		
I can use a range of words to qualify my opinions.		

Unit 5
It's not good enough

go to Useful language p. 83

Get ready to write

- Which of these goods and services have you complained about in the past?
  - service or food / drink in a restaurant ☐
  - accommodation, e.g. a hotel ☐
  - a public service, e.g. the post office ☐
  - public transport, e.g. a rail service ☐
  - products or service from a shop ☐
  - a financial service: bank, credit card company etc. ☐
  - a health issue: a doctor / hospital ☐
  - the repair or servicing of equipment, e.g. a car / TV ☐
  - other _____

- How do you prefer to complain? Rank these methods in order of preference (1 = the most preferred).
  - face-to-face ☐
  - telephone ☐
  - email ☐
  - letter sent through the post ☐

- Which method do you think is the most effective? Is this the same as your preferred method?

A letter of complaint

Look at examples

1 Read these three letters of complaint quickly, ignoring the spaces.
Which of the subjects in *Get ready to write* does each letter concern?

Letter 1 _____

Letter 2 _____

Dear Service Manager,

On 13 February, I had my car serviced at your city centre garage. ¹......

Driving to work yesterday morning, I heard a loud rattling noise coming from the engine. I stopped and phoned the breakdown service. The engineer who came out towed me home and advised me not to drive the car again until it had been looked at by a qualified mechanic.

In order to resolve this unsatisfactory situation, I suggest you collect the car from the above address and carry out another full service. ²......

I look forward to hearing from you and to a speedy resolution of this problem. I will wait for a week before seeking advice from my solicitor. Please contact me at the above address or by phone.

Yours faithfully,

Dear Mr Knightly,

On 27 April, I purchased a brand new Zoomasonic DVD recorder at your store in the new shopping mall.

I am now writing to complain that this recorder is faulty and therefore not fit for purpose. Although it is possible to play pre-recorded DVDs, it does not record from the television. Everything seems to be working, but when I try to replay the recording, the DVD is empty.

³...... As I have only had the product for two weeks, I am not prepared to have this equipment repaired.

I look forward to hearing from you and to a swift resolution of this problem.

⁴...... I should be very grateful if you would contact me at the above address or by phone.

Yours sincerely,

Letter 3 _____

Dear Mr Garrett

5 _____ As you may remember, I contacted you two months ago, in early March, to let you know that one of my windows was broken.

As the broken window has not been repaired, the flat is draughty and, consequently, my heating bill has risen. The wall below the window is also becoming damp, with the result that it will soon need redecorating.

6 _____ You are required by law to carry out any repairs within a period of four weeks of being contacted by a tenant.

I am keen to resolve this situation amicably, but I will have no choice but to contact the Housing Department of the local council if I do not hear from you within a week of the date at the head of this letter.

Yours sincerely,

3 Each of the three letters of complaint comprises four paragraphs. What is the purpose or topic of each paragraph?

Paragraph 1 _____

Paragraph 2 _____

Paragraph 3 _____

Paragraph 4 _____

4 All the letters are written in formal English. Find formal expressions in the extracts which have a similar meaning to these informal expressions. The number of the extract is in brackets.

a solve this problem (1) _____

b asking for advice (1) _____
c get in touch with me (1) _____
d I bought (2) _____
e doesn't do what it's supposed to (2) _____
f fast (1 and 2) _____
g the law says you have to (3) _____

h in a friendly way (3) _____
i looking after my flat (3) _____

j the worsening state (3) _____

2 There are two sentences missing from each letter. Read the letters again and find the missing sentences from this list. Write the correct letter in each gap.

a According to the terms of my tenancy agreement, the maintenance of the property is your responsibility.
b I am enclosing a copy of the documents relating to the original service.
c I am most disappointed because the service was not as thorough as it should have been.
d I am writing to remind you about the deteriorating condition of my flat.
e To resolve the problem I require you to either replace the faulty product or refund my money in full.
f Unless I hear from you within seven days, I shall be forced to take legal advice.

Did you know ...?

These are the most complained about goods and services in the UK. (The figures are percentages of all complaints made.)

– Mobile phones	6.7%
– Banks & other financial institutions	5.3%
– Internet service providers	4.6%
– Computer hardware and software	4.1%

Plan

5 You are going to write a formal letter of complaint.

a Think about how you would feel in the following situation.

You were a passenger on a train going from your home town to the nearest airport, where you were due to get on a flight to the United States. Even though you had allowed plenty of time for your journey, your train was delayed by several hours with the result that you missed your flight. The airline was unsympathetic and you had to buy another air ticket. When you arrived at your destination you had missed the first half of an important business meeting.

b In your notebook, plan a letter as if you were this rail traveller. Follow the same four-paragraph structure as the three letters you have read.

Focus on ...
avoiding repetition

1 When writing emails and letters it is advisable to avoid repeating the same words or phrases too often. Look at these common alternative ways of conveying similar ideas:

To resolve this problem	*In order to resolve this unsatisfactory situation*
	One way of dealing with this problem would be to
I am enclosing / attaching*	*Please find attached / enclosed …*
	Enclosed / Attached you will find …
Could you possibly …	*Please could you …*
	I would be (most) grateful if you could …
As you may remember,	*You will remember, …*
	May I remind you (that) …
Further to our discussion	*As (we) discussed earlier, …*
	With reference to our earlier (telephone) conversation, …
	Regarding our recent discussion, …

*We use *enclosed* in letters and *attached* in emails.

2 Think of alternative ways of conveying the ideas underlined in these sentences.

a <u>Please contact me</u> at the above address.

----

b <u>I shall expect to hear from you</u> within the next seven days.

----

c If I hear nothing, <u>I shall have no choice but to</u> contact my solicitor.

----

d <u>This letter is to inform you</u> that my flat was broken into last night.

----

e <u>I can now confirm</u> that I have taken legal advice regarding this matter.

Write

6 Write a first draft of your letter, using Letters 1–3 on pages 26–27 as models where possible. Write 150–180 words.

a Follow your paragraph plan.
b Write in formal language. Include as many of these features as you can:
   – formal expressions from Exercise 4 on page 27
   – full, uncontracted verb forms
   – expressions from *Focus on avoiding repetition*

Learning tip

If you are writing a formal, transactional letter, keep the tone serious and businesslike. Do not write any more than is necessary for your purpose.

Check

7 Read through your letter carefully, checking these points.

   – Is your language appropriately formal?
   – Is it clear what you are complaining about?
   – Is it clear what you want the other person to do?
   – Have you included any information which is not essential?

8 Write the final version of your letter, making any necessary corrections and improvements.

Class bonus

1 Exchange letters with a partner, then read carefully what they have written.
2 Write a reply to your partner's letter as if you were the rail company employee who deals with customer complaints. Answer all the letter's key points.

E✗tra practice

Rewrite these impolite or inappropriately informal extracts from letters of complaint.

a This is to let you know that if you don't sort this problem out, I'm going to get my solicitor on to you.

----

b It's not good enough – you said you'd phone me back the same day and you didn't.

----

c I'm not satisfied and I want to know what you're going to do about it.

----

d You probably don't remember, but a couple of months ago I phoned you about the TV I'd just bought from you. ----------------------------------

----

e Just give me a full refund, or else! -----------------

----

f This is the second letter I've written in the last two weeks. Are you going to reply or not?

----

g If I don't hear from you pretty soon, I'll be getting in touch with the police.

----

h If you care about your reputation, you'd better replace the fridge by the weekend.

Can-do checklist

Tick what you can do.

	Can do	Need more practice
I can write a formal letter of complaint.	✓	✓
I can avoid repetition when using formal language.	✓	✓
I can use a range of expressions appropriate to formal letters of different kinds.	✓	✓

1 You are going to hear a telephone conversation between a bank employee and a customer who is ringing about a complaint she recently made about the bank. The employee fills in a follow-up form as the customer is speaking, but makes a number of mistakes.

a Before you listen to the conversation, read through the partially completed form.

b ⊙3 Now listen to the conversation. Answer any unanswered questions and correct any errors. You may need to listen again.

2 Would you see the following at the beginning (B) or the end (E) of an email or letter? Write B or E in the spaces.

a *Best*   ------
b *Cheers*   ------
c *Good to hear from you* ------
d *Got the email – thanks* ------
e *Speak soon* ------
f *Take care*   ------

3 What do the following mean if they are used in an email?

a *BTW* ----------------------------
b *FYI* ----------------------------
c *IMO* ----------------------------

Customer complaints department Follow-up form

Date 15 July 2007

Customer details

Name Mr / Mrs / Ms   Elena O'Brien

Address 17, The Avenue, Potters Bar, Hertfordshire, EN16 4HM

Phone number 01707 888173

Bank account number --

Details of the complaint

1 Date of transaction or poor service

   Day 16   Month May   Year 2007

2 Date of first complaint?

   Day ---------- Month ---------- Year 2007

3 Contacts spoken to previously at bank

Brief summary of your complaint

On 16 April customer phoned to cancel a direct debit to electricity company.

On 15 June customer noticed that this regular payment to the electricity company had left her account as usual.

Customer phoned the bank and was told that cancellation would be actioned.

But money taken from account again in July.

Action taken

Report to General Manager. Recommend full refund + compensation payment to customer.

Someone should phone customer tomorrow.

4 The following shortened sentences are taken from personal letters and emails. If you were to write these sentences out in full, which word or words would you add to each sentence?

a (............) Glad to hear you had a good holiday.

b (............) Expect we'll see you when we get back.

c (............) Suppose I should have told you I was going to be late.

d (............) Heard anything from Jo recently?

e (............) Sorry – I meant to warn you about the loose handle.

5 You have just had a very long letter from an old friend you have not seen for several years. Your friend has told you what he / she has been doing since you were last in touch with each other. Unfortunately, you do not have the time to reply in full to the letter now, so write a very short letter. Include the following.

– Thank your friend for his / her interesting letter.

– Apologize for not being able to reply straightaway. Give a reason.

– Promise to write soon.

6 Rewrite this paragraph, which is in conversational language, using more formal language.

I'm just about to get my exam results which I'm pretty sure will be okay – not fantastic but not too bad. After that, who knows? I mean, I'd quite like to work for your company for a bit, but it all depends on what I'm doing two months from now.

----

7 Complete each of these sentences with two appropriate words.

a My ....firm........ / .... personal belief is that we should not allow this to happen.
[This person feels very strongly about something.]

b I .... / .... believe that this is not the way to do things.
[This person has a genuine belief that they are correct.]

c I feel .... / .... certain that things will get worse before they get better.
[This person is convinced that they are right.]

8 Read this email to the editor of a newspaper.

a Fill the gaps with appropriate words.

> Dear Sir
> I am writing in response [1]............... the editorial in last week's issue of your newspaper, in [2]............... the following statement appeared: 'We firmly believe that, if they [3]............... the choice, the residents of this town would prefer to do without street lights after midnight [4]............... to pay an extra ten percent on top of their already very high local taxes.'
> I am sure I am [5]............... the only reader who wants to dissociate themself from this statement. I feel absolutely certain that [6]............... a vote was taken tomorrow, the majority of residents would vote for the lights to remain on [7]............... the hours of darkness. The reason is simple. Over the past 20 years our town [8]............... turned into a dangerous place at night. If we want to make sure this situation does not get even worse, we must not make [9]............... any easier for would-be thieves and thugs. Switching off the street lights after midnight would, [10]............... any doubt, make this situation worse.
> Paulo Gonzalez (by email)

b Write a brief response to Paulo Gonzalez's email, expressing your own opinions on this subject.

9 Match these formal expressions with their informal equivalents.

a amicable   1 get in touch
b purchase   2 ask for / look for
c contact   3 looking after
d deteriorating condition 4 friendly
e fit for purpose   5 buy
f maintenance   6 worsening state
g seek   7 does what it should

10 Write the first paragraph of a letter reporting the loss of a suitcase by an airline you travelled with. You reported the loss in person before you left the airport, and you followed this up with a telephone conversation to the airline three days later. You are still waiting for someone to return your call.

Unit 6
This is my life

Get ready to write

○ On what occasions do people need a CV (curriculum vitae) or résumé?

○ What information would you include if you had to write your own CV now?
Choose from these categories of information.
  – Achievements and awards ☐   – Hobbies and interests ☐
  – Career history ☐   – Likes and dislikes in music, food, etc. ☐
  – Education history and qualifications ☐ – Specific skills: computing, languages, etc. ☐
  – Family background ☐

○ If you were reading someone's CV as an employer, what other information would you like to know in
addition to the categories of information above?

----

go to Useful language p. 83

Preparing a CV and covering letter

Look at examples

**1 Quickly look at the example CV on page 33.
Why do you think the writer has chosen to
start her CV with her academic achievements
rather than her work experience?**

**2 Read through the CV again and answer
questions a and b.**

  a Approximately what proportion of the CV consists of the
    writer's commentary on the factual information?
    a quarter / a half / three-quarters
  b How is the style of this commentary different from the
    rest of the information?

**3 In your notebook, list all the abbreviations
used in Sujin's CV and their meanings.**

  Example: DOB   *Date of birth*

**4 It is normal to write a covering letter to send
with your CV when applying for a job. Read
this sample covering letter written by Sujin.
What does it add to her CV?**

Dear Mr Freeman

I am writing in response to your advertisement in *The Times*
of 2 June 2007 regarding the post of Financial Adviser.
Please find enclosed my CV summarizing my education,
qualifications and experience.

I first became interested in finance and banking when I
worked as an administrative assistant at the Central Bank
in my home city of Seoul in South Korea. Although this was
a temporary position which lasted for only two months, it
made me realize that finance was an area I would like to
work in.

I am currently a trainee manager for a bank located in
central Manchester. This has been excellent experience for
me, as it has introduced me to the full range of banking
activities. However, I have come to realize that my main
interest lies in finance rather than in the everyday
management of a bank. I would now like to specialize in
providing financial advice to members of the public, because
I believe I have the qualities necessary to help people to
make those important financial decisions which affect their
lives. I take great interest and pride in keeping up-to-date
with general economic developments, as well as with day-
to-day changes in the money markets. I now feel that my
future lies in this field, and it is for this reason that I am
applying for the post you have advertised.

I would be available to come for an interview at any time.
I look forward to hearing from you.

Yours sincerely,

Sujin Lee

SUJIN LEE

Term-time address
Flat 7, 4, Nipper Lane,
Salford M3 7RH
Tel: 07958 765377
E-mail: sujin@student.manchester.ac.uk
DOB: 25/07/1982

Home address
81, Sokong-dong,
Chung-ku,
Seoul 100-070 South Korea

Nationality: South Korean

EDUCATION

2003–2006 The University of Manchester, United Kingdom
BA Econ (Hons) Business Studies and Economics – Result 2:1
Modules included: Business Management / Economics and Finance
Skills developed: Independent project work has developed my analytical thought, numeracy and
ability to manage projects.
Regular group work in small teams has improved my ability to build effective working relationships.

1999–2002 High School, Seoul, 'A' grades in English and Mathematics

WORK EXPERIENCE

July–Aug 2002 Central Bank, Seoul, S. Korea
Administrative Assistant

2006–2___ HPVR Bank (Manchester)
Trainee branch manager

ACHIEVEMENTS & AWARDS

Academic 2005 – Prize for highest grade in Economics and Finance module.
2001 – two awards for strong academic grades in Business and English language.

Societies *Manchester University Squash Club* – 2005 Captain of women's team. Leadership skills developed.
Community Action – organizing group outings and a Christmas party for elderly residents.
Financial and organizational skills involved.

Other activities Yoga: Instructor Adv. Level 3. I have run classes at a local adult education centre.

SKILLS

IT European Computer Driving Licence Certificate – competent in Microsoft Office packages including
Excel, Word, PowerPoint.

Languages Korean, Mandarin and English [IELTS Level 8]

INTERESTS

Travel I enjoy travelling to other countries and meeting people from different cultural backgrounds.
I have travelled widely in SE Asia and Europe.

Ambition To visit the US and Australia.

Sport Squash, yoga, swimming, walking, keep fit

REFERENCES

Academic Dr Harold Smith, Department of Business and Economics,
University of Manchester, Manchester M13 9PL
Tel: 0161 342 6768 / Email: H.Smith@manchester.ac.uk

Employer Mr Jin-Ho Lee, Human Resources Office, Central Bank, Seoul
747-9 Hannam 2-Dong, Yongsan-Gu, Seoul, 140-728, Korea
Tel: +82 2 797 1974 / Email: JH.Lee@centbank.com

Did you know ...?

Most postal addresses include the same information, but different nationalities write them in slightly different ways. Here are some examples:

Argentina

Juan Aguirre	recipient
Piedras No 623	street address / building
Piso 2	floor
C1070AAM Capital Federal	post code + city / town
ARGENTINA	country

Australia

Mr S. Tan	recipient
200, Broadway Avenue	house number / street address
WEST BEACH SA 5024	city / town / area + post code
AUSTRALIA	country

India

Mr I.K. Taneja	recipient
Flat 100	Number of apartment
Triveni Apartments	Apartment block
Pitam Pura	Area / suburb
NEW DELHI – 110003	City + post code
INDIA	Country

Plan

5 You are going to write a CV and covering letter for yourself. Complete exercises a–c.

a Start by collecting the factual information you need in your notebook. Use these headings:
  – Education (start with the most recent)
  – Work experience
  – Other useful/relevant experience
  – Achievements and awards
  – Skills
  – Interests

b Refer to the sample CV to check the kind of detail that the writer includes.

c Decide on the order you wish to present the information in.

6 Now collect and note down these details:

  – Addresses, phone numbers and emails of the people you are going to provide as references and any others that might be useful.
  – Dates – related to education, employment, etc.

Focus on ...
reducing full sentences to notes

It is important when writing a CV to be economical with language. You need to include full details without giving the person reading the CV too much to read. For this reason, we tend to write in note form rather than full sentences. Examples:

– *'A' grades in English and Mathematics* instead of *I achieved A grades …*
– *Kitchen and serving work (evenings and weekends)* instead of *I worked in the kitchen and served in the evenings and at weekends.*
– *Leadership skills developed* instead of *This work developed my leadership skills.*

Reduce these sentences to their essential details.

a I passed my driving test in 2007.

----

b I speak English fluently and my written German is good.

----

c I was awarded a Prize for the 'A' grade I achieved for my Business Management project.

----

d I gained a BA degree in Economics with Honours from London University in 2006.

----

e I was a member of a company working group which produced a report in 2006 entitled 'Staff–management communication issues'.

----

f Between October 2005 and January 2007, I worked as an assistant to the Head of Human Resources.

Write

7 You have decided to apply for the job described in this advertisement.

a Read the advertisement. How many of the qualifications and skills do you have?

AUSTRALIAN TOURS

is looking for a motivated Tour Guide for extended tours from Cairns to Cape York in northeastern Australia.

Successful applicants must have the following qualifications and skills:
- A clean driving licence (at least 3 years)
- Good people skills
- The ability to speak and write English (Intermediate level or above)
- First aid diploma
- Basic cooking skills
- Be prepared to work irregular times and be away from home for extended periods

On-the-job training will be provided.

To apply, send your current CV with a covering letter to the address below.

b Write a draft CV, including only information relevant to this job.

c Write a covering letter, saying why you are interested in doing this job, and giving details of any skills and qualifications you have that make you a suitable candidate.

Learning tip

Include only the information that is relevant to the job you are applying for.

Do not exaggerate your abilities – you may get caught out at your interview.

Check

8 Read through your CV and letter carefully, checking these points.

- Are your CV details correct and complete?
- Is the CV clearly formatted and is the language as concise as possible?
- Does your covering letter contain useful additional information and explain why you are suitable for this job?

9 Write the final version of your CV and letter, making any corrections or improvements.

Class bonus

1 Exchange completed CVs and covering letters and read what your partner has written.
2 Take turns to interview each other. Ask questions based on the information included in the CV and letter.

E✗tra practice

Find a job online or in an English language newspaper that you are interested in and qualified to do. Then do either **a** or **b**.

a Write a covering letter related to this job that you could send with your CV.

b Email the company asking for an application form and further details of the job.

Can-do checklist

Tick what you can do.

	Can do	Need more practice
I can write a CV.	✓	✓
I can write a covering letter to accompany a CV.		
I can reduce full sentences to notes.		

Unit 7
Private and confidential

Get ready to write

○ Reorder these words and phrases to make a definition of *job reference*.
an employee's character / a written recommendation / by a present employer
describing / future employer / skills and qualifications / to a possible

----

○ Answer these questions.
a Why do people need job references?

----

b Have you ever asked someone to write a reference for you? Or have you ever written a
reference for another person? What was the purpose of the reference?

----

c Did you, or the person you wrote the reference for, read the reference before it was sent?

go to Useful language p. 83

Writing references

Look at examples

**1 Read the extracts from two job references
on the opposite page. What are the main
differences between them?**

Did you know ...?

In the UK, references are usually given in
confidence. However, it is unusual for employers
to give negative references without clear verifiable
evidence, as unsupported negative comments
may be challenged – sometimes in law –
by employees.

2 Which of the two references ...
a provides more detailed information about Ben
    Sherwood? _2_
b is more formal? Underline examples. ......
c is written in note form? Underline examples. ......
d gives you a clearer picture of Ben Sherwood? ......
e would be more useful from the point of view of an
    employer? ......

Extract 1

Post GV 762/07 Reference for Ben Sherwood

I have known and worked with Ben Sherwood since he was first appointed at Global Systems in 2003. As a member of my department staff since 2004, he is someone for whom I have the greatest respect.

During his time at Global Systems, Mr Sherwood has been involved in a number of key projects which have contributed greatly to the international reputation of our company. Notable among these projects was his setting up and management of Project Peru, the success of which was largely due to Ben's commitment and leadership skills.

On a more general note, Ben is enthusiastic and dependable in everything he does. He has always shown flexibility and been prepared to take on any work asked of him, whether or not he has previous relevant experience. On a day-to-day basis, he is unfailingly good-natured and respectful to colleagues, whether they are above or below him in the management structure.

Reading the description of the job for which he has applied, I can honestly say …

Extract 2

Confidential – Request for Reference for Ben Sherwood

The above has applied for a job as Overseas Development Manager with us and has agreed that we can contact you for a reference. I would be grateful if you could provide whatever details you feel able to under headings 1–9 below.

1 The above person was/is employed with us as:
  International Project Offcer .... Dates: *Feb. 2002–* ....

2 General character
  Enthusiastic and reliable at all times. Has shown leadership skills and flexibility. Thoroughly honest and always good-natured.

3 Attitude
  Always positive. Willing to take constructive advice.

4 Relationships with others
  Excellent. Polite and respectful in dealings with colleagues at all levels within the company.

5 Team-working
  Excellent, both as team leader and team member.

6 Competence – state skills if appropriate
  Has the ability to analyze problems quickly and accurately and work out effective strategies for dealing with them.

7 Overall performance in past role(s) with your organization
  Absolutely first rate. Has always performed to the best of his ability.

8 Calmness under pressure

9 Any other …

Focus on ...
formal language in relative clauses

1 Circle the relative pronouns and underline the more formal relative clauses in these extracts from the two references. The first one is given as an example.

a he is someone for (whom) I have the greatest respect.

b Notable among these projects was his setting up and management of Project Peru, the success of which was largely due to Ben's commitment and leadership skills.

c Reading the description of the job for which he has applied, I can honestly …

2 Rewrite extracts a–c above with less formal relative clause structures.

a *he is someone who I have the greatest respect for.*

b _____

c _____

3 Rewrite these sentences in more formal language.

a It was a serious legal case whose details could not be made public.
It was a serious legal case, the details of which could not be made public.

b My colleague Juan is someone who I have always worked very well with.

_____

c That's a question there is not a single answer to.

_____

Plan

3 **You are going to write a job reference for someone you know well. He/She is applying for the job as tour guide on page 35. Choose a work colleague, a fellow student, or a friend. Complete exercises a and b.**

a Make notes under the following headings:
  – The person's particular skills and abilities ☐
  – Relationships with other people (colleagues/students) ☐
  – How you know the person / How long you have known him/her ☐
  – General character and attitude to work ☐
  – The person's current job, course or situation ☐
  – Past successes and achievements ☐

b Decide on the most appropriate order for these headings and notes. Write 1–6 in the boxes above.

Learning tip

When planning a reference, think about the following:
– Content – What information would a potential employer find useful?
– Structure – Decide whether to start with factual information – for example how long you have known the person, or subjective opinions – what you think of the person. Both are common reference formats.
– Style – References are normally written in formal language. Your reference may be read by many people, so a formal style is more appropriate.
– Impression – Think carefully about the overall impression you want your reference to leave: positive, negative or neutral. Neutral references may be regarded as negative.

Write

4 **Write the reference for the person you have chosen, using Extract 1 on page 37 as a model. Write 150–175 words.**

a Use all the information from the notes you have written.
b Write in formal language, using full verb forms and formal relative clause constructions where necessary.

Check

5 **Read through your reference carefully, checking these points.**

– Is the information you have included correct and complete?
– Is the language you have used formal?

6 **Write the final version of your reference, making any necessary corrections or improvements.**

Class bonus

1 Exchange references with another student.
2 Read the reference your partner has written and decide whether you would employ the person described or not.
3 Think of some questions you could ask the person described in the reference at an interview.
4 If you have time, role play the interview with your partner.

E✗tra practice

Write a reference in note form using the headings below. The reference can be for the same person you chose in Exercises 3–6 or for someone different. Use Extract 2 on page 37 as a model.

Confidential – **Request for Reference for (Name)** ....

1   The person's current position / course

   ....

2   Your relationship with the person, including length of time known

   ....

3   The person's general character and attitude

   ....

4   Relationships with other colleagues / students

   ....

5   The person's successes and achievements

   ....

6   The person's particular skills and abilities

   ....

7   Additional comments

   ....

   ....

Signed ....

Position ....

Date ....

Can-do checklist

Tick what you can do.

	Can do	Need more practice
I can understand the differences between different kinds of job references.	✓	✓
I can write job references in two different formats.		
I can use relative clauses in formal writing.		

○ Companies and other organizations often carry out surveys. What kind of organization might include the following questions in their surveys?

a

> Are you generally very satisfied, satisfied or dissatisfied with the punctuality of the service?

----

b

> The shelves are always well stocked.
> Agree ☐   Not sure ☐   Disagree ☐

----

c

> **Were all the rental charges explained clearly to you?** YES / NO

----

d

> Thinking about Departure services, please tell us if standards were **Above** expectations, **Met** expectations or were **Below** expectations in these categories:
>
> Check-in   _____
>
> Baggage screening   _____
>
> Queuing for security _____

----

e

> Which of the following best describes your circumstances? Are you ...
> 1 Registered unemployed and receiving benefit?
> 2 Not registered unemployed but claiming benefit?
> 3 In work – not claiming benefits?
> 4 In work (less than 16 hrs) – claiming benefits?

○ What other questions might be included in each organization's survey? Think of one more question for each organization.

go to Useful language p. 83

Did you know ...?

Paid surveys are online surveys where people who provide information are rewarded either by a cash payment or by being entered into a competition. However, there are also online survey scams where customers are falsely promised rewards in exchange for information. In one of these, the fraudulent organization collects and sells the information to interested companies but then closes their website without rewarding the people who provided the information. If you complete a survey, try and make sure you know it is for a reputable company.

A report

Look at an example

1 Read the report of a customer satisfaction survey on the opposite page and find the answers to these questions.

a Who were the customers in this survey?

----

b What, from the point of Fly-U-There, is the most important information to come out of the survey?

----

c What changes might improve the Fly-U-There service for two groups of dissatisfied customers?

Fly-U-There: Customer report

According to a recent customer satisfaction survey carried out by an independent market research organization, *Fly-U-There* is Europe's top airline in terms of quality. The survey was carried out in ten European countries between January and March 2006. Passengers were asked to rate 70 different airlines on a number of criteria. The results of the survey, in which more than 10,000 travellers took part, were analysed by computer and presented in a league table which gave an overall result that reflected the average customer satisfaction for each airline.

The criteria by which the airlines were judged included in-flight security, punctuality, assistance with problems, catering, comfort, and the quality of the in-flight and ground services. *Fly-U-There* was given an overall grade of 16.7 out of 20.

- _____

  The airline scored the maximum possible grade for punctuality and assistance with problems.

- _____

  Customers gave the airline 18 points for price in relation to quality of service. It was clear that a small number of users would be prepared to accept a lower standard of service in order to pay a lower price.

- _____

  Customers, asked for their views on relations with staff, commented favourably on the friendliness of both ground staff and cabin crew. There was some indication that for many, the efficiency and friendliness of *Fly-U-There* was the result of it being a comparatively small airline.

- _____

  While most passengers were very happy with in-flight comfort and the standard of catering, a small but significant minority found the seating cramped. The score for catering was 15.5 out of 20, an increase of 3 points on a similar survey carried out at the same time last year.

In response to recent independent market research, *Fly-U-There* is currently planning changes to its fare structure, which it hopes will attract more business passengers.

2 **The headings have been removed from the report. Complete exercises a and b.**

a Write four of the headings below in the correct spaces in the report.
- Advertising and Marketing
- In-flight comfort / Catering
- Punctuality / Assistance with problems
- Quality in relation to price
- Staff-passenger relations

b How do the section headings help the readers of reports like this?

----

3 **What is the purpose of the first two paragraphs of the report?**

----

4 **Complete sentences a–f with verbs from the box. There are similar sentences in the report. Use the past simple in the active or the passive voice.**

analyse	carry out	give
judge	score	take part

a A survey into patients' experiences in public hospitals ___was carried out___ by scientists from Harvard University last year.

b 25,000 patients _____ in the survey.

c Patients _____ the hospitals by the following criteria: cleanliness, medical care, the friendliness of staff, the standards of catering.

d The opinions of patients _____ by computer.

e Following the survey, the top hospital _____ a grade of 19.5 out of 20.

f 50% of hospitals in the survey _____ very low marks for their standards of catering.

Focus on ...
reduced relative clauses

Compare the underlined sections of these two sentences. How are they different?
- The article, <u>which was written by a university professor</u>, proves that human activity is causing climate change.
- The article, <u>written by a university professor</u>, proves that human activity is causing climate change.

The relative clause in the first sentence, which contains a passive verb, is shortened to a participle phrase in the second sentence (the relative pronoun 'which' and the auxiliary verb 'was' have been omitted). These phrases are sometimes called 'reduced relative clauses' and are common in written English.

1 Study the following extracts from the report. Underline the parts which could be expanded to form relative clauses, then rewrite the extracts with complete relative clauses.
- According to a recent customer satisfaction survey, carried out by an independent market research organization, …

- Customers interviewed during a flight seemed more satisfied than those who returned written questionnaires.

- Customers, asked for their views on relations with staff, commented favourably on the friendliness, …

----

2 Rewrite these sentences using reduced relative clauses.
a Most people who were questioned said they were very happy with the service.

----

b The questions, which were chosen at random, focused mainly on people's experiences over the last four weeks.

----

c The results which were produced by the survey show that only a small minority are seriously dissatisfied.

----

d The service, which was introduced last year, faced serious problems in its early stages.

Plan

5 You are going to write a report of a survey of supermarket customers. Look at the results of the survey, in which customers were asked whether they agreed or disagreed with these six statements about the supermarket itself. Then complete a–c below.

Statement	Agree	Disagree	Not sure
The shop is well laid out.	22%	69%	9%
Signs are clear and informative.	60%	25%	15%
The store is clean and tidy.	45%	45%	10%
The store has a pleasant shopping atmosphere.	61%	28%	11%
The store is easy to move about in.	17%	66%	17%
There is a sufficient number of checkouts.	9%	86%	5%

4,500 customers took part in this survey

a Complete these statements.
  1 28% of customers <u>felt the store did not have a pleasant shopping atmosphere.</u>
  2 22% of customers ....
  ....
  3 A very large majority of customers ....
  ....
  4 69% of customers ....
  ....
  5 Only 5% of customers ....
  ....
  6 Equal numbers of customers ....
  ....
b Which two areas or services are customers most satisfied with?
  ....
c Which two areas or services are customers least satisfied with?
  ....

Write

6 Write your report, using the example on page 41 as a model. Write 200–220 words.

a Use information from the supermarket survey on page 42. Choose the information you think is most important.

b Use formal language and incorporate reduced relative clauses where appropriate.

c Try to include some of the verbs from Exercise 4.

d Give your paragraphs clear sub-headings.

Learning tip

Check your report to make sure that you are not assuming that the reader already has knowledge on this subject.

Check

7 Read through your report carefully, checking these points.

– Is your language appropriately formal?
– Have you included the essential information?
– Are your paragraph sub-headings clear?

8 Write the final version of your report, making any necessary corrections and improvements.

Class bonus

1 Compare your report with the reports of other students. Have you selected and reported on the same 'essential information'?

2 Discuss this statement in pairs or groups: Customer surveys are just a gimmick to make us think that companies care about what we think. Their real motive is to persuade us to buy more of their products.

E✗tra practice 1

Complete these report sentences using your own ideas.

a According to a recent report carried out in my country, a significant majority of adults _____

b Nearly a quarter of all supermarket customers questioned prefer _____

c An increasing number of residents of my city/town believe that _____

d Over 50% of school students asked for their views on relations with their teachers said _____

e Only a small minority of people in my country believe that the government _____

E✗tra practice 2

You are going to write a report of a customer survey carried out in your town.

a Choose an organization you know something about. It could be a local company, a supermarket, a train service, etc.

b Make a list of the three or four criteria by which you think this organization should be judged. For example, if you choose a transport service, one of your criteria could be 'punctuality'. Look back at the report in Exercise 5 and think of your own ideas related to your chosen organization.

c From your own experience/knowledge, give scores out of 20 for the criteria you have listed,
e.g. *Punctuality* 17.

d Write your report in 150–200 words.

Can-do checklist

Tick what you can do.

	Can do	Need more practice
I can write a report in clear sections and include appropriate sub-headings.		
I can incorporate reduced relative clauses into my writing.		

Get ready to write

- Imagine you work for an online mail order business and you are looking for new items to add to your catalogue. Look at the four products below and decide which item would be most suitable for:

  men ....
  women ....
  children ....
  teenagers ....
  young adults ....
  families ....
  taxi drivers ....
  fitness enthusiasts ....

- Now imagine you are going to attend a presentation of one of these products. Think of one piece of information you would like to find out about each item.

  A ....
  ....
  B ....
  ....
  C ....
  ....
  D ....
  ....

go to Useful language p. 83

Notes on a presentation

Look at an example

A

How often has your mobile phone run out of power when you needed it most? This wind-up phone charger could literally save your life.

B

With this Satellite Navigation System you can take mobile calls safely while you drive!

C

Cycle and fold in just 20 seconds!

D

Ever wanted to run at unbelievable speeds or jump amazingly high? Now you can with

P-O-W-E-R-I-Z-E-R-S !!!!

1 Read these notes, which are a record of a product presentation someone attended. Which of the four items on page 44 do these notes relate to? ································

MODELS

1 ª ································ 2 Professional

Occasional user ᵇ ································

TARGET CUSTOMERS

Men ✓ / women ✓ / Teenagers ᶜ ············· / Children ᵈ ···········

KEY FEATURES

High-speed running: ᵉ ············· kilometres an hour

Jump very high: ᶠ ············· metres

Practical and leisure use: Getting to work / ᵍ ···················· /

ʰ ···················· / competitions / clubs

SUITABILITY FOR OUR CUSTOMERS

PROS	CONS
For all adults: Men and women	Not suitable for ⁱ ····················
Easy to put on	Need for protective clothing:
	knee pads, ʲ ····················
	and ᵏ ····················

RECOMMENDATIONS

Stock demonstration models only: one of each

Include in next catalogue - Extreme Sports Equipment section

Clear safety warning!!

2 Read the notes again. They consist of

– a note-taking framework (set of headings)
– detailed notes about the product (with some information missing)
– recommendations for action

Which of the above do you think was written …
a during the presentation?
································
b before the presentation?
································
c after the presentation?
································

3 ⚫14 Listen to the product presentation and add any more information you can to the notes in Exercise 1.

Did you know …?

In a recent survey into people's online shopping habits, 35% of people surveyed said that the main reason they shopped online was to avoid crowds. The next most important reasons were:
– lower prices
– the ease of comparing products and prices
– to avoid having to travel to shopping areas
– a wider choice of products

Plan

4 You are going to a product presentation on headphones which block out external noise.

Fed up with outside noise?
Keep it out with these
headphones.

In your notebook, write a note-taking framework to help you listen for the information you want to find out at the presentation. Use the framework on page 45 for ideas, and keep the questions below in mind.

– How much do the headphones cost?
– What kind of people would be most likely to benefit from buying these headphones?
– What are their special features?
– How user-friendly are they?
– What are the pros and cons for likely customers?

Are there any other questions you would like to know the answer to?

Learning tip

If you know in advance what kind of information to listen for, you can write a note-taking framework to complete while you are listening.

Write

5 🔊**5** **Listen to the presentation and complete your framework with appropriate notes.**

Check

6 **Read through your notes carefully, checking that they are complete. Listen to the recording again to make sure you did not miss any important points.**

7 **Could you give your own presentation to colleagues based on the notes you have made? If not, what else would you need to include?**

Focus on ...
noun phrases

In order to save time, noun phrases are often used in notes instead of complete sentences. Here are some examples from the notes on page 45.

occasional user	[It is suitable for people who want to use it occasionally.]
high-speed running	[It enables you to run at high speeds.]
practical and leisure use	[It can be used for practical or leisure purposes.]
good safety record	[It has a good safety record.]
need for special clothing	[Special clothing is needed.]

1 Reduce these sentences about the product above to short noun phrases.

  a This electric coffee maker makes espresso.
    <u>electric espresso maker</u>
  b This model can make two cups.

  c This model is fully programmable.

  d It has a handle which is heatproof.

  e The deluxe model cleans itself.

2 Reduce these sentences about other products to short noun phrases

  a It has a guarantee for three years.

  b This bulb lasts for ever and is ultra efficient.

  c It has a battery which runs on water power.

  d This memory stick has a capacity of 2GB.

  e This kit will help you survive on any camping holiday.

Class bonus

1 Work in groups of three or four. Take turns to make mini presentations of the noise-cancelling headphones to the rest of your group.
2 As you are listening to your classmates' presentations, note down any differences you hear between what they are saying and the original recording.

E✗tra practice

Imagine you are going to give a product presentation for one of the products below.

a Choose the product you would like to present.

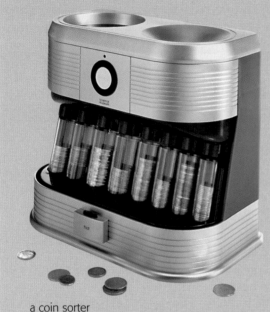

a coin sorter

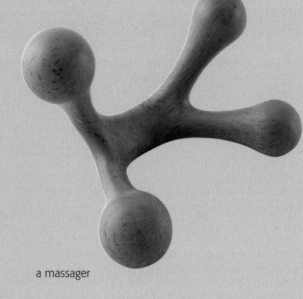

a massager

b Write a set of notes to refer to if you were going to present the product
   to a group of people who know nothing about it. Think about the following:
   – What kind of people will your product appeal to?
   – What are its special features?
   – How much does it cost?

Can-do checklist

Tick what you can do.

	Can do	Need more practice
I can write a note-taking framework.	✓	✓
I can take notes from a product presentation.	✓	✓
I can reduce complete sentences to noun phrases.	✓	✓

Unit 10
I'll email you

go to Useful language p. 83

Get ready to write

- Which of these problems associated with sending and receiving emails in the workplace do you think are the most serious? Rank them in order of importance (1 = most serious, 6 = least serious).
  - Receiving spam or junk emails ☐
  - The pressure to reply to emails as soon as you receive them ☐
  - The quantity of emails received at work due to being copied in on correspondence between other people ☐
  - The trend for emails to replace phone conversations and face-to-face meetings ☐
  - Employees' use of their workplace computers to send and receive personal emails ☐
  - Management by email, for example, employees being told by email that they have lost their job. ☐

- Imagine these emails had just arrived in your inbox. Which would you open and which would you delete?

⬇ Inbox (11)

From	Subject
✉ Easy cash	Need cash now?
✉ John Dexter	Hi, it's John
✉ Hot Date	Love only a click away
✉ Human Resources	Next week's meeting
✉ Finance Dept.	Funding update
✉ Charles P	Salary query
✉ Digi World	Confirmation of order PX97238
✉ Sue Edwards	Your travel tickets
✉ National Bank	New account information
✉ FreeMoney	There's loads of it
✉ :-)	Be my friend

Work-related emails

Look at examples

1 **One of the key features of emails in the workplace is that they are usually concise and to the point. Most writers do not write more than they need to. Read emails 1–4 on the opposite page and complete a and b.**

a Which email contains the least unnecessary information? ......

b Underline the words, phrases or sentences that you think could have been omitted from the other emails.

2 **What do you notice about the style of emails 1–4? How are they different from personal emails and from letters? Think about the following:**

- beginnings and endings

- the structure of the email

- sentence construction and length

- the degree of formality

Did you know ...?

- It is estimated that over 40% of emails sent are actually spam, and this percentage is increasing every year. Despite many warnings, more than one in four people respond to spam emails at least once.

- The city of Boca Raton, in Florida, is known as the 'spam capital of the world', since a very high proportion of all spam emails come from addresses there.

1

Dave,

Thanks for looking at the figures – you're quite right, those two small amounts were errors – entirely my fault. From the end of this month we are launching a large new e-commerce store at the site that automates the calculation of sales information and payments – so the manual aspect will be entirely removed.

We've grown really quickly and the new store software will take us to the next level – look out for an announcement during this month.

Cheers,

Joe

3

Dear Conference Member,

Renate has asked me to email you to check that you will not be attending the evening meal on Thursday 17 May. This is because you have elected to leave the conference before 8.00 pm on that day.

We apologize for the fact that the times of meals may not have been made clear in our original conference invitation.

Regards,

Melanie Dean

2

Dave,

Your payment arrived in our account today. I'll have your order picked up by DPD tomorrow morning. It should reach you by Friday. Let me know if it arrives in good order, please.

Regards,

James Roland
Printer

4

Joe,

Please send the electronic report again. It's not opening on my computer for some reason.

Thanks.

Chris

PS Have a good holiday if I don't see you before.

Plan

3 You are going to write two work emails, one in response to an email you have received and one related to a telephone conversation with a colleague. Read this email from a colleague. Make notes in response to each question Nick asks you.

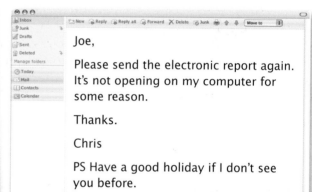

Hi,

Trying to arrange a meeting for latter half of next week. We'll need at least 3 hours. What days and times are you free Wednesday to Friday? Thursday morning's no good for John.

Agenda will include the following:

1 personal use of Internet by employees – a complete ban?
2 possible future move of head office out of city centre – where?
3 introduction of flexitime working – Yes/No decision

Any immediate thoughts on any of these? Anything you want to add?

Will tidy up wording and send final agenda ASAP.

Regards,

Nick

4 **16** **Listen to this phone conversation and imagine you are the person who received the call. Make any notes you will need in order to write your second email. The first two notes have been made for you.**

Notes

• Kate – email Ed   • Late – here 12 o'clock
•

Class bonus

1 Working with a partner, compare the notes you have made after listening to the telephone conversation.
   – Is the information in both sets of notes the same? (Check the correct facts in the *Audioscript* on page 93).
   – Have you noted down the same main points?
2 Decide which information to include in your email.

Write

5 **Write the two emails, using the notes you made. Remember these features of effective work-related emails:**

   – the importance of being concise
   – sentences should be short and clear and need not contain unnecessary information
   – simple beginnings and endings – there is no need for the level of politeness associated with traditional letters.

Focus on ...
short simple sentences

If you need to convey a simple message, it is often more effective to write in short sentences, rather than long sentences containing one or more subordinate clauses. Compare these email extracts with their longer equivalents.

> Please resend your electronic report. The first one is not opening on my computer.

> Please could you send me your electronic report again, as the first one you sent is not opening on my computer.

> Your payment arrived in our account today. I'll have your order picked up by DPD tomorrow morning. It should reach you by Friday.

> Thanks for your payment which arrived in our account today. If I can manage to have your order picked up by DPD tomorrow morning, it should reach you by Friday.

In your notebook, rewrite these long sentences as a series of short simple sentences suitable for email, omitting any unnecessary words or information.

a I apologize for the delay on this payment, but there were a number of coding errors which made it impossible for our system to process the invoice you sent us.

b Following a useful conversation with a member of your staff this morning, I am now writing to confirm that we wish all our savings to be transferred from our Gold Account to the new Direct Savings Account.

c We notice from our records that you have not yet returned the grant application form which was sent out to you on 10 November. We would remind you that if you wish your application to be considered for the next academic year, your form will need to be returned to us at the above address by the end of this week.

Check

6 Read through your emails carefully, checking these points.

– Are your messages clear?
– Are your emails concise enough?
– Do they contain any unnecessary information?

7 Write the final version of your emails, making any necessary corrections and improvements.

Learning tip

You can use abbreviations, acronyms or emoticons if you are sure the person who receives the email will understand them. Examples:

- Abbreviations: *etc.* / *viz.* (See Useful language Unit 12 – p.84)
- Acronyms: *BTW* / *FYI* (See Language focus Unit 2 – p.16)

Warning!
It is better not to use smileys or emoticons like these: ☹ / ☺ / :-) in formal emails. Keep them for very informal personal emails.

E✗tra practice 1

Rewrite this traditional letter as a concise email.

Dear Jeremy

Following on from our telephone conversation of this morning, we are now writing to confirm that we wish to go ahead with the order of a new photocopier for our office. Having discussed two possible models, we can also confirm that we require model OC850/C2 – that is the colour model.

We would be grateful if you could let us know an approximate delivery date as soon as possible.

With best wishes,

E✗tra practice 2

You wrote the email below, but have now decided that a letter would be more appropriate. Rewrite the email as a formal letter.

Renate,

Sorry, working lunch planned for 21 Aug is now off. Possible new dates: 27 Aug, 3 or 12 Sept – all at 9.30 a.m.

Let me know asap dates you could make and which is best for you. Hope to confirm by weekend or Monday at the latest.

Sorry again,

Can-do checklist

Tick what you can do.

	Can do	Need more practice
I can understand the main differences between traditional letters and emails in work-related contexts.		
I can write work-related emails using clear, simple language.		
I can incorporate abbreviations and acronyms in emails when appropriate.		

Unit 11
This is the course for me

○ When applying for a course of study at a university or college, students are expected to write a personal statement in addition to completing an application form. Have you ever written a personal statement to support an application? If so, what was the most important information it contained?

○ Read through these tips advising students how to write a good personal statement. Fill the gaps a–p with the missing verbs. The first letter of each verb is given.

○ Which do you think are the most important tips? Is there anything you would add?

----

go to Useful language p. 83

Writing a personal statement – ten tips

General advice

1 Use black ink or type to ª*write* your statement.

2 ᵇP_____ on a separate sheet first, until you are happy with it.

3 Don't forget to ᶜk_____ a copy of the final version.

4 ᵈM_____ sure that your statement is well-structured, grammatically correct and that there are no spelling mistakes.

5 ᵉS_____ yourself. University admissions tutors are looking for well-rounded individuals, people with a real interest and motivation.

Specific advice

6 ᶠS_____ by saying why you have applied for this course. ᵍS_____ that you have done some research into the course you are applying for. ʰR_____ to particular aspects that appeal to you.

7 ⁱM_____ any academic qualifications or experience you have in relation to the course.

8 ʲW_____ about your interests and hobbies in and out of school. But don't ᵏi_____ everything you have ever done.

9 Don't just ˡl_____ what you have done; ᵐe_____ what you have ⁿg_____ from the experience.

10 Finally, ᵒs_____ what you hope to gain from ᵖa_____ ing this university or college.

A personal statement

Look at an example

1 **Read the personal statement on the opposite page, ignoring any errors, and answer questions a–c.**

a What does this applicant hope to do when she finishes her education?

----

b What level of education does she already have?

----

c What subject(s) does she think her studies to date will help her to teach?

Carla Pacione
Personal Statement

1   I have a variety of experience of working with young people in both academic and non-academic situations. Throughout my undergraduate course, I undertaken voluntary work at the local infant school. I found this very enjoyable and rewarding, as I often helped groups of less able children with specific tasks and found it very satisfing to see them begin to make progress.

2   In addition to my academic study, I have a number of interests. I play tennis, and badmington to a reasonable club level and have recently taken up rock climbing. I also love reading and going to the theatre.

3   When I was working on a summer play scheme, I took responsibility for a larger group of children aged 8 to 12 for a whole day, thoroughly enjoying the experience. I also recently acompanied a group of Year Six pupils from Milan on a week-long English-language coarse in Scotland. Both these experiences influensed my decision to specialize for Upper Primary teaching. I felt I could really stimulate and communicate with this age group and found the feedback I recieved from the children very rewarding. There is many other factors which could be useful in my future career. I was captain of my school tennis team between the ages of 10 and 12; my mother and father are both teachers here in Italy, and I was always very interested in watching any TV programmes about teaching and education.

4   In selecting the Postgraduate Certificate in Education at edinburgh, I am making a concious choice of a course which will challenge and test me to the full. Your course has a formidable reputation in the training of primary school teachers.

5   My first degree course, which was a BA in Philosophy, was largely text-based and involved writing regular essays, thus utilizing my written language, research and analytical skills. The emphasis on moral, social and political issues have increased my awareness of a variety of contemporary debates, thereby equipping me to tackle themes relevant to the classroom, such as social skills and equal opportunities. The content of my course will assist me in contributing to a wide range of school curriculum areas, in particular Citizenship, History and English, all of which are backed up by my own school-level qualifications.

Did you know ...?

This table shows the percentages of young people entering higher education in the top ten countries.

New Zealand	76%	Norway	62%
Finland	72%	Iceland	61%
Sweden	69%	Hungary	56%
Poland	67%	Netherlands	54%
Australia	65%	Korea	49%

These figures are from an OECD report for the year 2001.

2 Read the statement again and answer questions a–e.

a How far does the writer of this statement follow the tips in *Get ready to write*? ....
....

b Should the paragraphs be reordered? ....

c Is there any information that is unnecessary? Underline it.

d Is there any information that could be added? ....
....

e Is the style sufficiently formal for a statement of this kind? ....
....

3 Read the statement again carefully. Identify and correct the errors. (There are nine spelling errors and four errors of grammar.)

Focus on ...
writing complex sentences

One of the features of formal language is the use of complex sentences, which have a main clause and one or more dependent clauses. For example: *I found this very enjoyable and rewarding* (main), *as I often helped groups of less able children with specific tasks* (dependent).

The clauses in complex sentences can be linked in various ways:
– by conjunctions: *as / if / when / because*
– by relative pronouns: *which / who / where / whose*
– by using participle clauses: *Arriving late, I …*

1 Find examples of the different kinds of dependent clauses in complex sentences in Carla Pacione's statement on page 53.

2 Rewrite these groups of short sentences from student statements as single complex sentences in your notebook.
   a I think I am well suited to a career in law. This is partly because I enjoy studying social issues in today's society. I also believe I have the skill to use factual evidence to present a persuasive argument.
   b I think my contributions to class discussions have improved. This is probably due to the fact that I have developed my knowledge of the subject. This has in turn made me more confident about speaking in front of the whole class.
   c My personal experience of journalism started when I was very young. My father wrote for a magazine. He often took me with him when he went to interview people for his articles.

Class bonus

1 Working with a partner, compare how you have rewritten extracts 2a–c in *Focus on writing complex sentences* section.
2 Choose one of the statements and discuss other ways of rewriting them as a single sentence. You can reorder the information as well as using conjunctions, relative pronouns and participle clauses.

Plan

4 🔊 **17** **You are going to write your own personal statement to support an application for a higher education course. Listen to two extracts from a radio programme describing university degree courses. Decide which course you would like to apply for.**

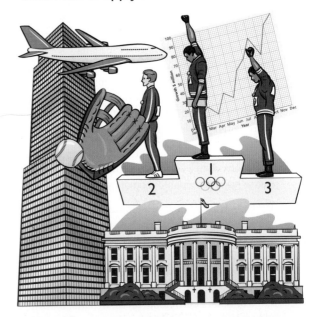

5 🔊 **17** **Listen again and make notes in response to these questions about the course you have chosen.**

Questions	Notes
What appeals to me about this course?	
What qualifications or experience do I have that make me a suitable applicant for this course?	
What interests or hobbies do I have that are relevant to this course?	
What would I hope to gain from the course?	

6 Now plan your personal statement, paragraph by paragraph, following the advice given in the tips in *Get ready to write*, and referring to the notes you have just written.

Write

7 Write your own first draft personal statement, following your plan and using complex sentences where appropriate. Use the improved and corrected version of Carla Pacione's statement as a model. Write 200–225 words.

Check

8 Read your draft statement carefully, checking these points.

- Content
  Have you followed the advice given in the tips in *Get ready to write*?
  Have you shown interest and enthusiasm for the course you have chosen?
- Structure
  Have you started by saying why you are interested in following this course?
  Have you started a new paragraph for each new topic?
- Style
  Is your style sufficiently formal? Have you used complex sentences?
  Have you checked your spelling and grammatical accuracy?

9 Write the final version of your personal statement, making any necessary corrections and improvements.

E✗tra practice

Rewrite this paragraph taken from another personal statement to improve the sentence structure and accuracy.

I first became interested for composition during my 16+ school exams. Composition is now my muscicle passion. This passion is reflected in my ambitions. These include composing for films, television and radio. In addition to my studies, I spending a considarable amount of my free time compose.

I am also study English and Music Technology at school. These subjects, along with music, helps another of my ambitions. This is to right a musical.

Learning tip

When writing about yourself, try to avoid sounding big-headed or over-confident. Find ways of expressing interest and enthusiasm rather than saying how brilliant you are at something. Use phrases like these:
- *Maths has intrigued me for many years.*
- *I believe this course will satisfy my curiosity about the world around us.*
- *From an early age I have been fascinated by the workings of the human body.*

Can-do checklist

Tick what you can do.

	Can do	Need more practice
I can write a personal statement in formal, accurate language.		
I can express interest and enthusiasm without sounding over-confident.		
I can edit and correct inappropriate or incorrect language.		
I can write complex sentences incoporating a number of clauses.		

Unit 12
Listen and take note!

Shall I write a list?

- In which of these situations have you made or would you make written notes?
    - while watching a TV programme or listening to a radio programme ☐
    - while listening to a university lecture or academic talk ☐
    - at a commercial presentation of a new product ☐
    - while listening to a political speech ☐
    - before going shopping ☐
    - while playing a phone message left by someone ☐
    - while interviewing someone ☐

- Think about these questions.
    - a What special difficulties are associated with making notes while someone is speaking?

    - b If you had the opportunity, would you make an audio or video recording of a lecture or presentation to listen to later? Why / Why not?

    - c Why might it be easier to make written notes from a recording than while someone is speaking?

    ----

go to Useful language p. 84

Making notes

1 🔊 You are going to listen to a talk about happiness. Listen to Part 1. What do you find out about the rest of the talk?

Look at an example

2 Read these notes someone made on the first part of the talk, then answer questions a–c.

a What devices has the note-writer used – for example, symbols, abbreviations, capital letters, etc.?

----

b How easy are the notes to follow and understand?

----

c 🔊 Is there anything you would add to the notes? Listen again and check.

HAPPINESS – result of scient. research

8 factors affect hap.

1 MONEY + hap.

   a Mon. CAN make you hap. -> rich happier
      than poor

   BUT N.B.

   b Comp. wealth v. imp. to peop. Happier if
      richer than friends.

2 DESIRE + hap.

   Peop. who desire much more they have –

   LESS hap.

   ∴ – LIMIT desire

Plan

3 Do you have any special techniques for writing notes? If you had written notes on this part of the talk, how would they be different?

----

4 Here are some of the skills associated with making effective written notes from a talk, speech or presentation. Rank them in order of difficulty, with 1 being the most difficult.

- Selecting the most important points to note. ☐
- Being able to condense or rephrase what the speaker is saying. ☐
- Writing quickly – using abbreviations and other symbols. ☐
- Organizing your notes clearly using headings, underlining, highlighting, etc. ☐
- Revising your notes soon after you have written them to correct, expand or clarify what you have written. ☐

5 Before you listen to Part 2 of the talk about happiness, write any numbers, letters or headings you think will help you structure your notes. (Remember the lecturer has already said that he will be considering 'eight factors'; in the first part he has dealt with the first two of these, and in the third part he will deal with factors 6–8.)

Write

6 🔘 Listen to Part 2 and make notes, using some of the devices mentioned in Exercise 2a, in the framework you made in Exercise 5.

Check

7 Read your notes carefully, checking these points.

- Can you understand your notes?
- Which note-taking devices did you use?
- Check your notes against the *Audioscript* (see page 94)

8 Rewrite your notes, making any necessary corrections and improvements.

Did you know ...?

'Speedwriting' is a system for writing quickly that was developed in the 1920s at the University of Chicago. Unlike shorthand, which is based on symbols and marks, speedwriting uses the normal letters of the alphabet, but shortens words by leaving out silent letters and short vowels. The following line is written in speedwriting: .flo lin s wrtn n spedwri\ Because it uses only half the letters, speedwriting is over twice as fast as longhand. Although it is not as fast as shorthand, regular users can write at an average speed of about 100 words a minute.

9 🔘 **10 One way to make effective notes is to prepare a plan before you listen. One example of a good plan is to divide your paper into the sections below:**

'Key points' column Only write here after you have made main notes. Use this column to write very brief reminders.
'Main notes' area Make full, meaningful notes in this part of the page.
'Summary' area Summarize each page of your notes here.

Look at how the notes from Part 1 of the talk have been written in this format below. Then listen to Part 3 of the talk and complete the Key points and Main notes for factors 6–8.

KEY POINTS	MAIN NOTES
8 factors	Happiness — result of sci. research
1. MONEY —	1 Money + hap
✓(?)	a Mon. can make you hap. → rich happier than poor
	BUT — N.B.
	b Comp. wealth v. imp. to peop. Happier if richer
	than friends.
	2 DESIRE + hap.
	Peop. who desire much more than they have —
2. DESIRE — ✗	LESS hap.
	• LIMIT desire

SUMMARY
Individual happiness depends on a variety of internal and external factors.

Focus on ...

selecting and noting key words, and paraphrasing

Other approaches to note-writing are to include only key words and to paraphrase.
Example:
Elderly ~~people are on average just as~~ happy as ~~the~~ young, ~~and actually~~ rate themselves more satisfied with ~~their~~ lives ~~overall~~.

Notes:
· Elderly happy as young
  [Old no more unhappy than young.]
· Rate themselves more satisfied with lives
  [Judge themselves more content with lives.]

1 Cross out any words you could omit from this extract from the talk.

  In a study of 2,727 people aged between 25 and 74, researchers found that other things such as gender, personality type and social factors affect how you feel as you get older. For instance, both men and women tended to experience more positive emotions as they aged.

2 Make notes using only the important words from this extract.

3 Paraphrase your notes where possible.

Learning tip

Constructing a mind map – a diagram showing how ideas relate to each other – can be a useful technique if you want to condense or reorder your ideas. There is no right or wrong way of drawing a mind map. Each individual will show their understanding of ideas in a slightly different way.

Factors affecting happiness

Birth

Intelligence

Money

Can buy happiness BUT
Most people want more money than their friends

Desire

More desire = less happiness

∴ we should limit desire

Class bonus

Work in pairs or small groups. Discuss the ideas below. How far do you agree or disagree with them?
– Money can buy happiness.
– People are more concerned with comparative status than with absolute wealth.
– There is no connection between intelligence and happiness.
– Extroverts tend to be happier than introverts.
– Married people are happier than single people.

E X tra practice 1

Check the effectiveness of your note-making:
a After a few days, reread your notes on Part 2 or Part 3 of the recording.
b Expand the notes into a piece of connected writing as similar as possible to the original recording.
c Compare your writing to the *Audioscript* for recordings 9 and 10 on page 94.

E X tra practice 2

🔊 11 Listen to a short talk about social status. Write notes under these headings.

KEY POINTS	MAIN NOTES

SUMMARY

Can-do checklist

Tick what you can do.

	Can do	Need more practice
I can listen to a talk or lecture and select key points of information.		
I can write notes quickly and economically, omitting words, using symbols, abbreviations and other visual devices.		
I can organize notes clearly using numbers, letters and bullets.		
I can select key points from written notes.		

Get ready to *write*

- Match these words with their meanings 1–3 below:
  a handout ☐
  b presentation ☐
  c seminar ☐

  1 (*noun*) a document given to students or reporters which contains information about a particular subject
  2 (*noun*) an occasion when a teacher or expert and a group of people meet to study and discuss something
  3 (*noun*) a talk given to a group of people giving information about a new product or idea, or piece of work

- Have you ever given or listened to a presentation during a seminar in an educational or a work situation? If so, answer these questions.
  a Who gave the presentation? _____
  b What was the subject? _____
  c How long did it last? _____
  d Was the presentation accompanied by visuals and/or a handout?

  _____
  e What were the best and worst aspects of the presentation?

  _____

- If you were asked to give a 15-minute presentation tomorrow on anything you wanted, what subject would you choose?

  _____

Preparing a presentation

Look at an example

1 An effective presentation involves speaking naturally, not reading a script word for word. However, one way of preparing a presentation is to write notes to remind you what to say at each stage of your talk.

Read the notes on the opposite page. They have been written on five separate prompt cards: one for each section of a presentation you are going to listen to. Put the cards into what you think is a logical sequence by numbering them 1–5.

Card ......

ADVERTISERS' MOTIVATION in showing this image of men

- not to amuse!
- to appeal to women by making them strong
- strategy successful at first but now negative effect
- women do not want to look cruel

Card ......

CONCLUSIONS > THANKS > QUESTIONS?

- advertisers! flatter women BUT don't insult men
- new car commercial: save man and car!

Card ......

INTRODUCTION TO SUBJECT

- men and women in TV commercials – changing image
- Advertisers' reason for this image

Card ......

PUBLIC REACTIONS TO COMMERCIALS

- Men's complaints up x 10 – commercials offensive not funny
- Survey 1000 adults – results:
  women – intelligent / caring but sometimes aggressive / cruel
  men – weak / lazy / incompetent

Card ......

TWO EXAMPLES

- man + girlfriend back to untidy flat – phones cleaners not police
- man about to fall on to car – woman saves car not man

2 ⊙12 **Listen to the presentation and check the sequence you predicted in Exercise 1.**

3 **The cards have been designed to make it easier for the speaker to give the presentation. Look carefully at the cards and answer questions a–d.**

a Which words are written in capital letters? Why?

----

b Which words are highlighted? Why?

----

c How are bullet points used?

----

d What kinds of words are used and not used on the cards (nouns, verbs, etc.)?

----

4 **Design a card to help you give the first part of a presentation on one of these subjects:**

- Why I like/dislike TV commercials
- My favourite TV commercial or TV programme

Class bonus

Work with a partner. Take turns to give the first part of your presentation, referring to the card you have just made.

5 Look at this handout which the speaker has prepared to accompany the presentation in Exercise 2. What are the similarities and differences between the handout and the speaker's prompt cards?

Men in television commercials – a changing image

1   How has men's image changed?

1.1 Men now portrayed in negative light in TV commercials, in contrast to women.

1.2 Two examples
- Young man takes new girlfriend back to very untidy flat. To save face, man pretends flat has been burgled. Instead of phoning police, he phones flat-cleaning service.
- Man falls out of window and hangs on by fingertips, over street above parked car. Woman sees, says "Hang on!" BUT, instead of helping man, she drives car away to prevent damage.

2   Public reactions to these images

2.1 Increase (x10) in complaints about commercials from men.

2.2 New stereotypes offensive, not funny.

2.3 Results of survey of 1000 adults
- men portrayed as weak, lazy and incompetent
- women seen as intelligent and caring, but very assertive, aggressive or even cruel.

3   Motivation of advertisers

3.1 To flatter women by making them stronger than men.

3.2 Initially this strategy successful, but now has negative impact, because women do not want to appear aggressive or cruel.

4   Conclusions

4.1 Advice to advertisers: flatter women but don't insult men.

4.2 Remake car advert – save the car and the man.

Did you know ...?

In the USA today, TV advertising is regarded as the most effective type of mass-market advertising. For this reason, the cost of advertising on prime-time TV can be astronomical. One 30-second commercial spot during the annual Super Bowl football game, which is watched by an audience of 90 million, costs nearly $3 million.

Focus on ...
omitting unnecessary words

When writing notes, prompt cards or handouts, it is common to leave out articles, determiners, possessive adjectives and other words that do not directly affect the meaning. This saves space and focuses attention on key words and ideas.
<u>Underline</u> any unnecessary words in this short extract.

<u>A</u> television commercial, often called an advert in the UK, is a form of advertising in which goods, services, organizations, and ideas are promoted via the medium of television. Most commercials are produced by an advertising agency, and airtime is purchased from a TV channel or network.

Plan

6 You are going to plan a presentation and write an accompanying handout. Choose one of these titles as the subject of your presentation:
- A current social trend in my country
- The education system of my country
- Competition between supermarkets in my country
- How other nationalities see my country and its people

7 Write notes in preparation for producing a set of prompt cards which you could refer to if you gave the presentation on your chosen subject. Start with an introduction to the subject and end with a brief conclusion.

Write

8 Write a set of prompt cards for your presentation.

- Refer to the notes you made in Exercise 7.
- Use the sample cards as models.
- Use capital letters, bullets and highlighting.
- Keep the language on the cards concise and to the point.

9 Write a handout to accompany your presentation.

Learning tip

A handout should cover the same ideas in the same sequence as the presentation it relates to. It should be clear and concise, and it needs to be detailed enough to remind the reader about the content of the presentation.

Check

10 Read your prompt cards carefully, checking these points.

- Does each card follow on logically from the previous one?
- Would your cards enable you to give an effective presentation?

11 Write the final version of your prompt cards, making any necessary corrections and improvements.

12 Read carefully through your handout checking your these points.

- Is it clear and concise?
- Does it contain enough information to remind people of the main points of your presentation?

13 Write the final version of your handout, making any necessary corrections and improvements.

E✗tra practice

Imagine that this is a paragraph from an essay that you are going to convert into a presentation.

a Write a prompt card that you could refer to while giving this part of the presentation.

Perhaps the most significant change in the way young people communicate with each other in recent years has been the increasing use of text messaging. Whereas in the past, the most popular form of communication was the telephone – first the conventional landline, and then the mobile phone – today it is not uncommon for children and teenagers to send or receive 100 or more text messages every day.

b Now write the corresponding section of a handout.

Can-do checklist

Tick what you can do.

	Can do	Need more practice
I can write prompt cards to refer to during a presentation.		
I can write a handout to accompany a presentation.		
I can use various devices to highlight key features of a presentation.		

Unit 14
To sum up

○ Re-order these words and phrases to make the definition of the word *summary*.
but not / of something spoken / a short account / the details / the important points / which gives / or written

----

○ Which of the following could be described as types of summary?
  – news headlines – in newspapers or on the radio or TV
  – the blurb on the back cover of a paperback novel
  – a short story in a magazine
  – a newspaper account of a scientific report
  – an essay done by a school or university student

○ Think back to the last time you read or wrote a summary:
a What kind of summary was it?

----

b Why did you read or write the summary?

  – an entry in a diary
  – extracts from a long political speech
  – notes a student made while listening to a lecture
  – a chapter in a school textbook
  – a radio report of a sporting event

go to Useful language p. 84

Summarizing an article

Look at an example

1 **Read the article on the opposite page from the magazine *Scientific American*. Which of the following would make the best title for the article?**

  1

  | Archaeologists discover disease in ancient DNA |

  2

  | Mummies' DNA reveals origins of ancient disease |

  3

  | Leishmaniasis originates in North Africa |

2 **Reread the article. Highlight the key facts, then put brackets round unnecessary details. The first paragraph is done for you as an example.**

Did you know ...?

The substance we now call DNA was first identified in 1869 by the Swiss biologist Johan Friedrich Miescher. Miescher described it as a weak acidic substance in white blood cells.

In 1928, a British doctor called Franklin Griffith discovered that genetic information can be transferred from dead bacteria cells to live ones, proving that genetic material (DNA) can survive death.

In 1953, two biologists, the American James Watson and the Englishman Francis Crick, discovered the structure of DNA.

[Centuries of silence cannot keep ancient mummies from sharing their secrets with scientists. From archaeologists determining cultural practices to chemists studying embalming, mummies have revealed libraries of information.] Now such mummies are also yielding evidence about the diseases of the past by giving up the facts encoded in their preserved DNA, and new research may have established the ancient origin of a modern disease.

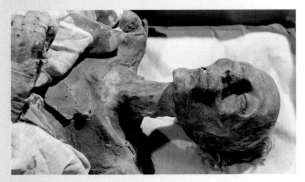

Leishmaniasis – a disease caused by microscopic parasites, like malaria, and transmitted by sand flies – results in painful skin sores and, in its most vicious form, causes at least 500,000 deaths worldwide every year. Today it affects communities in many parts of the world. The lethal form – visceral leishmaniasis, also known as black fever – is particularly prevalent in North Africa.

Albert Zink of Ludwig-Maximilians University in Munich and his colleagues tested the DNA of bone samples from 91 ancient Egyptian mummies and 70 from Nubia – modern Sudan – to determine if they had suffered from leishmaniasis. In 9 of the 70 Nubian mummies, taken from graves stretching as far back as AD 550, DNA of the parasite was discovered, proving the disease was endemic at least that far back. It is highly probable that it has even more ancient origins: four of the Egyptian mummies carried the parasite's DNA, each dating from the Middle Kingdom period of 2050 to 1650 BC, when trade ties with Nubia were strongest. Egyptian mummies from prior and later periods showed no sign of the disease.

In addition to highlighting the old cultural ties between Egypt and Nubia, it also adds further weight to the theory that visceral leishmaniasis first developed in Nubia. And the technique has been applied to other diseases, such as tuberculosis and malaria, to trace their development. 'We can contribute to a better understanding of the evolution of infectious diseases and, thereby, to a more efficient treatment and control of those diseases,' Zink says. The infections and viruses that proved a curse to ancient mummies may yet provide a cure for ancient scourges that still plague humanity.

3 **Read this summary, which is a third of the length of the original article. Complete a and b.**

 a Does it include all the key facts that you highlighted? ....
 b Does it leave out all the unnecessary detail that you put in brackets? ....

Researchers have discovered information about past diseases by analysing DNA from ancient mummies. Today leishmaniasis, which causes 500,000 deaths annually, is found in many parts of the world. The deadly type, visceral leishmaniasis, is found mainly in North Africa.

The researchers tested DNA of bone from Egyptian and Nubian mummies. They found leishmaniasis DNA in nine Nubian mummies from 550 AD, and in four Egyptian mummies from 2050 BC, when Egypt had strong trade links with Nubia. Egyptian mummies from before and after these dates showed no signs of visceral leishmaniasis. Researchers concluded that the disease developed in Nubia.

This research should help us to understand the development of other diseases, and how to control and treat them. [116 words]

4 In addition to leaving out unnecessary details, the summary also paraphrases some of the language in the original article. How have the following examples of original language been paraphrased in the summary?

Original	Summary
a evidence about the diseases of the past	1
b 500,000 deaths worldwide every year	2
c The lethal form … is particularly prevalent in North Africa	3
d trade ties with Nubia were strongest	4

Plan

5 You are going to write your own summary of a scientific article. Read this article, highlighting the key facts and putting brackets round unnecessary detail.

Focus on …
this, that, they, them and **it**

Words like *this*, *that*, *it* and pronouns (*they*, *them*) can be used to refer back, to avoid repetition and to make sure your summary reads fluently and is not just a sequence of disconnected sentences.

1 What do the words and phrases in italics in these extracts from the summary in Exercise 3 refer to?
  a *They* found… _____
  b … before and after *these dates* _____
  c *This research* should … _____
  d … to control and treat *them*. _____

2 Look at these pairs of sentences. In each pair, the second sentence is disconnected from the first. Change the second sentence so that it follows more fluently.
  a Malaria is an infectious disease, common in tropical and subtropical parts of the world. Malaria is spread by female mosquitoes.
  b Malaria infects between 300 and 500 million people every year and causes up to 3 million deaths. Most deaths which are caused by malaria occur among young children.
  c Experts claim malaria is a huge public health problem. Experts say malaria is a cause of poverty.

Jurassic 'beaver' is largest early mammal yet

A new fossil from China proves that the mammals that lived during the Jurassic era were more diverse than previously thought. The 164-million-year-old creature, known as Castorocauda lutrasimilis had a tail like a beaver, the paddling limbs of an otter, seal-like teeth and probably webbed feet. And although most Jurassic mammals discovered thus far were tiny, shrew-like animals, C. lutrasimilis would have weighed approximately a pound. Roughly the size of a small, female platypus, it is the largest mammal from this time period on record.

Chinese archaeologists led by Qiang Ji of Nanjing University found the well-preserved fossil, including impressions of soft tissue and fur, in Inner Mongolia. Other fossils had hinted that mammals might not just have been small terrestrial creatures until the demise of the dinosaurs 65 million years ago, but the beaver-tailed animal definitively pushes back the date of mammalian adaptation to an aquatic lifestyle by at least 100 million years. 'Based on its relatively large size, swimming body structure, and anterior molars specialized for fish feeding, Castorocauda was a semiaquatic carnivore, similar to the modern river otter,' the team writes in the paper announcing the find in today's issue of *Science*.

The discovery also highlights how little is known about early mammals. Most are represented by teeth and jaws alone. 'We stand at the threshold of a dramatic change in the picture of mammalian evolutionary history,' argues mammalogist Thomas Martin of the Senckenberg Institute in Frankfurt, Germany in an accompanying commentary. 'The potential of fossil-rich deposits in Liaoning Province in China or in Inner Mongolia is only just beginning to be exploited.'

6 Write the key facts you have highlighted in your own words, paraphrasing the original language where appropriate.

Write

7 Write a first draft of your summary in 90–100 words, using the paraphrased key facts you selected from the original. Use pronouns and other reference words and phrases to ensure that your summary reads smoothly.

Learning tip

To show that you have understood a text or an article, it is important to paraphrase the original language and to combine information in different ways from the original text.

Check

8 Read your summary carefully, checking these points.

 – Does your summary include all the key facts you highlighted?
 – Have you used your own words as far as possible by paraphrasing?
 – Have you combined information from the article in different ways?
 – Have you used reference words and phrases to ensure that the summary hangs together?

9 Write the final version of your summary, making any necessary corrections and improvements.

E✗tra practice 1

Try shortening your summary by reducing it to about 80 words. This may mean further paraphrasing or re-combining of information.

E✗tra practice 2

Reduce this text to 45 words.

The American crayfish is bigger and more aggressive than its European relatives and is pushing them to extinction.

But the behaviour that makes US signal crayfish so successful is now being used to stop their advance. Male crayfish are attracted by the natural chemicals used by females to attract a mate. But instead of mating, the crayfish are being removed from the river by scientists.

At a conference yesterday scientists from across Europe discussed the new technique for controlling the crayfish, which have escaped into rivers and lakes after being imported for restaurants.

The largest signal crayfish in the world, which was recently taken from a British river, weighed 200g.

[110 words]

Class bonus

Have a class competition. Who can reduce their summary to the smallest number of words? How few words can you use without losing essential information?

Can-do checklist

Tick what you can do.

	Can do	Need more practice
I can distinguish between key information and unnecessary detail in written texts.		
I can write a summary in my own words by paraphrasing original text language.	✓	✓
I can use pronouns and other reference words and phrases to ensure that a summary coheres.		

Unit 15
In my view

go to Useful language p. 84

Get ready to write

○ Answer these questions.
- a When and why do people write essays?
- b What was the last essay you wrote? Who read it?
- c If your last essay received a mark, what were the reasons for the mark you were given?
- d What do you find most difficult about writing essays, in your language and in English?

○ Which of these are features of a *discursive essay*?
- – a sequence of events ☐
- – arguments for and against an idea ☐
- – facts and figures ☐
- – the writer's opinion ☐

○ Imagine you have been asked to write an essay. Put these eight writing stages into the best order.
- – Find information on the subject, for example from a library or the Internet. ☐
- – Write a paragraph-by-paragraph plan for your essay. ☐
- – Check your language, spelling, punctuation and style, then correct if necessary. ☐
- – Work out what the essay question means and think about your own views on the question. ☐
- – Write your final essay. ☐
- – Organize relevant information and your ideas on the subject. ☐
- – Write a first draft. ☐
- – Check exactly what you have to do and how much to write. ☐

A discursive essay

Look at an example

1 Read these two discursive essay questions A and B. If you had the choice, which of the two would you answer?

2 Read the first paragraph of the essay on the opposite page quickly. Which of the two questions – A or B – does it answer?

3 Read the rest of the essay and write a sentence summarizing the writer's point of view.

A

The environment is increasingly under threat from human activity. Some people believe that it is the responsibility of governments to solve this problem. Others think the primary responsibility lies with individual citizens. What is your opinion?

B

The competing demands of work and family life are directly responsible for increasing levels of stress in the modern world. To what extent do you agree or disagree with this statement?

Did you know ...?

Worldwide, work-related stress costs business billions of dollars annually. Employment experts have estimated that 60%–90% of medical problems are associated with stress, and that as much as 45% of a company's profits can be spent on health benefits. 46% of workers reported that their jobs were 'very stressful'.

It has been estimated that unmanaged stress increases the risk of cancer and heart disease more than either smoking or high-fat foods.

¹Studies and personal observations show that stress is increasing in today's world. It is a commonly held view that this is due to the competing demands made on people by their jobs, family commitments, financial worries and other pressures.

²I will start by examining some of the present-day pressures on people. Money is undoubtedly a major concern for many people. Everyone needs enough money to feed, clothe and provide accommodation for themselves and their family. It is human nature for people to want to do the best they can for themselves and their families. This sometimes makes people choose a particular occupation, accept anti-social working conditions, which may include night working, or take on uncomfortably high levels of responsibility. These factors will lead to stress in some people.

³Families, however, need more than financial security. Husbands and wives, parents and children need to develop their relationships by spending time together. Shortage of time frequently causes stress. In my country, for instance, many people live in overcrowded cities and spend almost all their time working. If they have no time to relax with their children, tensions may arise between family members and this can cause stress.

⁴Despite these facts about the modern world, there are people who succeed in achieving a proper balance between work and family life. In my opinion, they do this by managing their time efficiently and by limiting how far they allow their jobs to interfere with their home life.

⁵In conclusion, I would say that people become stressed because they are unable to achieve an appropriate balance between the demands of work and their family commitments.

4 Read the essay again and do these exercises.

a Write the correct paragraph number next to each heading.
   - Overwork can lead to relationships being neglected ☐
   - People agree that stress is on the increase and understand the reasons ☐
   - The importance of a balanced lifestyle ☐
   - People need to be financially secure ☐
   - Time management is the key ☐

b Which expressions from the box below does the writer use …
   1 to say how they are going to begin their discussion of the subject?

   ----
   2 to give opinions – their own or those of other people?
   ----
   3 to talk about possibilities?
   ----
   4 to show that the essay is coming to an end?
   ----
   5 to introduce an example to back up an argument?

> for instance
> I will start by examining
> I would say that
> In conclusion
> In my opinion
> It is a commonly held view that
> (tensions) may arise
> this can cause (stress)

c How would you describe the style of the writing: formal or informal?

Plan

5 🎧13 You are going to write your own discursive essay, expressing your views on a different issue. First listen to a radio news item highlighting the issue. What is the topic under discussion? What different views do people have about this subject? What is your personal view? Make notes.

6 You are going to answer question A from Exercise 1. Read the question again and then complete a and b below.

a Work through the first two writing stages suggested in *Get ready to write*.

b Plan your answer paragraph by paragraph, using your own ideas and any other relevant ideas you have heard or read.

Class bonus

1 Write three sentences which contain the following:
 – a list
 – a subordinate clause at the beginning of a sentence
 – an adverb phrase at the beginning of a sentence
 – a non-defining relative clause.
2 Leave out all the commas, but include other punctuation. Exchange sentences with a partner. Add the commas to your partner's sentences.

Focus on ...
punctuation – the use of commas

Commas are often used in the following places.
– between items on a list:
 *I have three sisters, two brothers, four cousins and a nephew.**
– after a subordinate clause at the beginning of a sentence:
 If people take on too much work, they can become stressed.
– before and after words or phrases which interrupt the flow of a sentence:
 Children, on the other hand, need quality time with their parents.
– After adverb phrases at the beginning of a sentence:
 In my view, people spend too much time at work these days.
– Before (or before and after) a non-defining relative clause:
 I find my job, which involves travelling long distances, very tiring.
* A comma is sometimes added before 'and' in a list. This is particularly common in American English: *We travelled to France, Italy, Spain, and Germany.*

1 Find examples of these uses of commas in the sample essay.

2 Add commas where necessary to the following sentences.
 a All along the route we could see beautiful wooded gorges shimmering lakes silvery rivers and majestic waterfalls.
 b The Windy Islands which are north of Sicily are fantastic. If you are near enough stop there for a while.
 c Suddenly out of the blue one of three boys walking towards me rushed up to me shouted something I couldn't hear and grabbed my bag in which I had all my valuables: my wallet my mobile phone my camera and my return train ticket.
 d From what I have seen of the documentaries some of the most beautiful shapes and colours of the world are found in plants fish and other organisms that live on the seabed.

Write

7 Write the first draft of your essay.

– Follow your paragraph plan.
– Include some of the expressions from the box on page 69.

Learning tip

When you have decided on the opinions to include in an essay, think of convincing reasons and clear examples to back up these opinions.

Check

8 Read your essay carefully, checking these points.

– Have you answered the question fully, putting both sides of the argument and expressing your own views clearly?
– Have you followed your paragraph plan, starting with an introduction and ending with a conclusion?
– Have you used sufficiently formal language?
– Your grammar, spelling and punctuation (especially commas) correct?
– Have you written too many or too few words?

9 Write the final version of your essay, making any necessary corrections and improvements.

E X tra practice 1

a Write a summary of your essay in 100–110 words. Refer back to Unit 14 for help with writing summaries.
b Write an essay in answer to this question.
The ability to speak more than one language is essential in the modern world. How far do you agree or disagree with this statement?

E X tra practice 2

a Add the correct punctuation to the following paragraph.

the everglades stretch for hundreds of swampy miles across southern Florida home to hordes of snakes, alligators and assorted creepy-crawlies but now an invasion by deadly giant pythons is threatening the eco-system of the famous park

b Look at the rest of the text. Decide how many paragraphs it should be divided into and where the paragraph divisions should come.

The pythons, which are thought to have been released into the wild by careless pet owners, are no ordinary snakes. They are Burmese pythons native to South Asia and can grow 6 metres long, weigh 100kg and live for 20 years or more. The pythons have established breeding pairs in the swamps and are racing to the top of the food chain, even getting rid of alligators, which were previously the top predator in the Everglades. 'It is a very serious issue, especially as we have found breeding pairs and clutches of eggs. That means they've adapted to living here and they are having a big impact,' said Linda Friar, an official at Everglades National Park. The snakes are a serious threat to indigenous wildlife due to their big appetites and expansive tastes.

Can-do checklist

Tick what you can do.

	Can do	Need more practice
I can plan, structure and write a discursive essay.		
I can express my ideas and opinions formally in writing.		
I can use commas appropriately in formal English.		

Unit 16
According to statistics

Get ready to write

○ Look at the three graphic illustrations. Match each illustration with its correct name:
a bar chart / a pie chart / a line graph

 A   B   C

○ Which form of information do you find easiest to understand – a set of statistics, a graph, or a text? Why?

○ If you had to present information in a written form about the population figures for your town over the last ten years, which form would you choose? Why?

----

go to Useful language p. 84

A report based on statistics

Look at an example

1 Look at the bar chart below, which shows the unemployment rates in four European countries by country and by year.

a What do the two colours represent?
b What general trend does the chart show?
c What significant exception to the general trend is there?

Unemployment rate by country and year

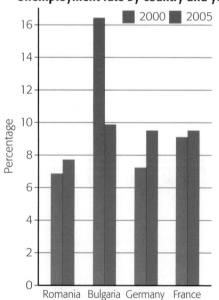

2 Look at the table of figures for employment rates in Europe in 2005 opposite.

a Which countries had the highest and the lowest employment rates?
b Write sentences comparing Malta with Luxembourg and comparing Belgium with the Netherlands.

Employment rates in Europe 2005

Country	%
Belgium (BE)	61.1
Czech Republic (CZ)	64.8
Denmark (DK)	75.9
Germany (DE)	65.4
Estonia (EE)	64.4
Greece (EL)	60.1
Spain (ES)	63.3
France (FR)	63.1
Ireland (IE)	67.6
Italy (IT)	57.6
Cyprus (CY)	68.5
Latvia (LV)	63.3
Lithuania (LT)	62.6
Luxembourg (LU)	63.6
Hungary (HU)	56.9
Malta (MT)	53.9
Netherlands (NL)	73.2
Austria (AT)	68.6
Poland (PL)	52.8
Portugal (PT)	67.5
Slovenia (SI)	66.0
Slovakia (SK)	57.7
Finland (FI)	68.4
Sweden (SE)	72.3
United Kingdom (UK)	71.7

3 Read this extract from a report on unemployment.

a How does information presented in this report compare with the bar chart and the table of statistics on page 72? What can a report do that the other forms of presentation cannot?

b Make a note of the ways in which the report writer refers to the following:

1 Upward or downward movements

----

2 Exact or approximate numbers

----

c Which adverbs does the writer use to qualify the upward or downward movements?

Plan

4 You are going to write a report based on another bar chart. Look at the chart below and answer these questions.

a Which item has seen a slight fall in its occurence in homes between 1998–99 and 2004–05?

----

b Which item has seen the highest rate of growth in its occurence between 2004–05 and 1998–99?

----

c What general trend does the chart show?

The trend in the employment rate is broadly flat. The trend in the unemployment rate continues to increase and the number of people claiming benefits has risen slightly. The trend in the inactivity rate continues to fall. The number of job vacancies has fallen slightly. Growth in average earnings, both excluding and including bonuses, has fallen.

The employment rate for people of working age was 74.5% for the 3 months ending in September 2006, down 0.1 over the quarter and down 0.3 over the year.

The number of people in employment for the 3 months ending in September 2006 was 28.99 million, up 56,000 over the quarter and up 192,000 over the year. Total hours worked per week were 925.4 million, down 0.9 million over the quarter but up 1.3 million over the year.

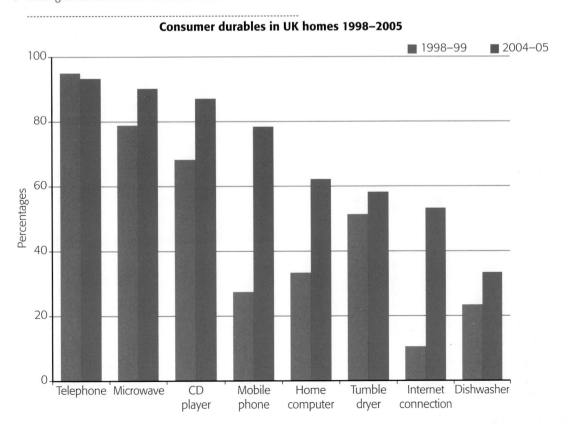

Consumer durables in UK homes 1998–2005

■ 1998–99   ■ 2004–05

Focus on ...

ways of referring to statistical trends and movements

Match these phrases with the figures they refer to.

1 slight increase   a 10:30
2 a massive fall   b 27%
3 a rise of fifty percent   c 30%
4 approximately a third   d from 150 to 137
5 just over a quarter   e from 2.7 to 2.8
6 down by nearly ten percent   f from 200 to 300
7 a ratio of three to one   g from 435 to 109

5 Plan the report you are going to write, based on the chart on page 73. Make brief notes in your notebook under these headings.

- Introduction: Point out the main trend(s).
- Three short paragraphs: Focus on three items that you consider significant or particularly interesting.
- Final paragraph: Make a comparison.

Write

6 Write your report, referring to your planning notes, and including some of the language used to refer to increases and comparisons from Exercise 3 and from the Focus on section. Write 200–250 words.

Check

7 Read through your report carefully, checking these points.

- Have you only included information from the chart and not added any ideas or interpretations of your own?
- Is the style of your language appropriately formal?

8 Write the final version of your report, making any necessary corrections or improvements.

Did you know ...?

In the same way that blind people use braille to read words, they can use tactile graphic images to obtain information that sighted people get from looking at diagrams, maps and pictures. A blind geography student, for example, can use a tactile map to learn about a particular terrain. Tactile graphics can be made from thermoform (a kind of plastic) or 'swell paper' on to which black and white images can be transferred as raised images by means of photocopying.

Class bonus

1 Design and conduct a survey for your class. Choose a subject that everyone finds interesting: for example, favourite kind of music, career ambitions, preferred holiday destinations.
2 Collate the results.
3 Write a brief report, drawing attention to the main results and making relevant comparisons.

Learning tip

When you write a report based on statistics, make sure your conclusions are drawn from the data and not your own ideas.

E✗tra practice

Write sentences about the information in this table. Example:
The total number of people employed in the 20–24 age group was almost double the number employed in the 15–19 age group.

United States – Active labour force for 15–19 and 20–24 age groups: 2000/2004 comparison

Age group	Gender	Year	Active persons
15–19	Female	2000	4,051,000
		2004	3,498,000
	Male	2000	4,317,000
		2004	3,616,000
	Total	2000	8,368,000
		2004	7,114,000
20–24	Female	2000	6,788,000
		2004	7,097,000
	Male	2000	7,558,000
		2004	8,057,000
	Total	2000	14,346,000
		2004	15,154,000

Can-do checklist

Tick what you can do.

	Can do	Need more practice
I can write a structured report based on information presented in tables and graphic form.	✓	✓
I can use a range of expressions to refer to statistical trends and movements.	✓	✓

1 What abbreviations are commonly used for the following?

a International English Language Testing System

----

b Bachelor of Arts _____

c Date of birth _____

d Honours (degree) _____

e Doctor _____

f Economics _____

2 Reduce these full sentences to notes.

a I have extensive experience of business management practices.

----

b My long-term aim is to set up my own company.

----

c I gained a first-class honours degree in biology.

----

d My recent work has included the development of new computer software.

----

e My ambition is to be the manager of a major company by the age of 30.

----

f I have attended courses in Business Management on a regular basis.

----

g In my spare time, I organize holidays and other activities for children with special needs.

----

3 Read this advert for a job in your city. Write the covering letter to accompany an application form related to the job.

Trainee Education Officer

The city museum service has a vacancy for a Trainee Education Officer.

The majority of your time will be spent providing overseas visitors with access to information about the city and our region. You will work in the museum and at sites of historical interest in the area.

Required Skills:
- You must have a proven interest in and a wide knowledge of our city and the surrounding area.
- You must be able to speak English and to understand normal spoken English.
- You should have a higher qualification in history, or a related subject.

Please complete the attached application form and send it with a covering letter to the address below.

----

4 Match these character adjectives with their meanings.

a *dependable*   1 able to change or be changed easily
b *enthusiastic* 2 never lying or cheating
c *flexible*   3 showing good manners to other people
d *good-natured* 4 can be trusted or relied upon
e *honest*   5 pleasant, kind or cheerful
f *polite*   6 showing keenness or great interest

5 Write a short reference for a friend or colleague. Make sure that you answer these questions.

– How long have you known this person?
– How do you know him/her?
– What is this person's current job or situation?
– How would you describe this person's good points?
– What are his/her achievements, qualifications and skills?
– How well does this person get on with other people?

6 Rewrite these informal sentences in more formal language.

a The people I'm writing to are all ex-colleagues.

b The employee I'm writing this reference for has worked for the company for over ten years.

c The projects he's been involved in have all been successful.

d The colleagues he's worked with here all speak very highly of him.

7 Rewrite these formal sentences in less formal language.

a The computer on which I am working is absolutely state of the art.

b Brad Ellis is the manager to whom we are responsible.

c Gerry is someone for whom I have the greatest respect.

d The meeting to which you are referring took place on 17 June.

8 The company which runs the bus services in your town has commissioned a customer survey. Write a short report based on these results.

	Customer response		
	Very satisfied (%)	Satisfied (%)	Not satisfied (%)
Comfort on bus	31	35	34
Punctuality of buses	16	64	20
Politeness of driver	65	30	5
Cleanliness of vehicle	25	40	35
Quality of driving	70	20	10

9 (114) **Listen to a product presentation and complete these notes.**

```
Item        _____

Models    • _____

          • _____

Suitable for • _____

Plus points 1 _____

          2 _____

          3 _____

Price     • _____
```

10 **Rewrite these sentences using reduced relative clauses where possible.**

a   Members of the public who were invited to take part in the survey were all sent a personal letter of thanks which was written by the Head of Research.

   ----

b   The survey forms, which were completed online, were analyzed by a group of sociologists who were specially trained for the purpose.

   ----

c   The results which were published in the newspapers represent just a small proportion of the data which was collected in the survey.

   ----

11 **Rewrite each of these sentences from a letter as two short sentences suitable for an email. Use direct language and omit any unnecessary information.**

a   I am organizing a party at the Octane Club for my best friend whose 18th birthday is on 30 April next year, and am looking for a suitable band for the evening.

   ----

b   I am writing to ask whether your band would be available to play at this event and, if so, please could you let me know how much you would charge for playing from 8 o'clock until midnight.

   ----

12 **Rewrite these sentences from the first draft of a personal statement replacing the underlined words and phrases with more formal language. (You may also need to change the word order.)**

a   *I'm really interested in doing this course because I've always loved learning languages.*

   ----

b   *I got 'A' grades for German and French and a 'C' for Russian. I've also been to all three countries for holidays, and so have often practised speaking.*

   ----

c   *We've also got satellite TV at home, which can pick up foreign channels, so I try to watch French, German and Russian programmes as often as possible.*

   ----

d   I've got penfriends in all three countries too and do my best to use their languages, but their English is really good, so we end up using English most of the time.

   ----

13 Imagine you are a student applying for the scholarship below. Write the covering letter mentioned in the scholarship advert under the heading 'Applying'.

English Language Scholarships

We have recently introduced English Language Scholarships for international students who are applying to study for a Research Degree at our university.

Are you eligible?

To be considered for a scholarship, you must meet the following requirements:

- You must have studied English Language for 5 years or more and have passed recognized examinations in the subject.
- You must have been accepted on to a course of higher study at the university.

Applying

To apply for a scholarship, complete our application form and send with a covering letter, explaining why gaining a scholarship is of particular importance to you.

14 Listen and make notes on this extract from a lecture about how to save money. Before you listen, remind yourself of the different ways of making notes in Unit 12 (pages 56–58).

----

15 Write a set of notes based on this extract from a talk. Start by crossing out any words you can safely omit. Make notes using only important information from the extract.

> Researchers from three universities interviewed 20,000 people over a 2-year period to produce the most in-depth study to date of this kind. Most of the findings were what researchers had predicted, but attitudes towards the future were surprising. Of the 5,000 people under the age of 30, a large majority (79%) said they were generally pessimistic about the future. Of those over the age of 60, 70% said they felt optimistic or very optimistic about the future.

----

16 Reduce this paragraph to a few notes which would help you to give a presentation to a group of fellow students.

> Babies are born with basic sensory capacities, for example vision and hearing, which are refined and developed throughout childhood. At birth babies can distinguish between different visual forms – new-born babies get bored and look away when they have been shown the same visual stimulus for some time, and only look again if a new visual stimulus is presented.
>
> Within a few days of birth babies learn to recognize their mother's face – they will look at a picture of their mother's face longer than a picture of a stranger's face. Similarly, young babies will listen to their mother's voice longer than a stranger's voice. There is even evidence that babies recognize their mother's voice at birth, from hearing the muted but still audible sounds in the womb. Although basic sensory capacities are present at birth, babies require continual sensory stimulation throughout the first few years of life for their sensory systems to develop normally.

17 Write a brief handout to accompany your presentation. Write only as much as would be needed by someone who had attended your presentation.

18 <u>Underline</u> the key points in this paragraph taken from a book about language, then write a summary of the paragraph in 50–60 words.

> The question 'Why do we use language?' seems hardly to require an answer. But, as is often the way with linguistic questions, our everyday familiarity with speech and writing can make it difficult to appreciate the complexity of the skills we have learned. This is particularly so when we try to define the range of functions to which language can be put.
>
> 'To communicate our ideas' is the usual answer to the question – and indeed, this must surely be the most widely recognized function of language. Whenever we tell people about ourselves or our circumstances, we are using language in order to exchange facts and opinions. This is the kind of language that will be found in reference books – and in any spoken or written interaction where people wish to learn from each other. But it would be wrong to think of it as the only way in which we use language. Language scholars have identified several other functions where the communication of ideas is an irrelevant consideration. Such functions include 'emotional expression' and 'social interaction'.

----

19 Join these groups of sentences using pronouns or other reference words.

a Many birds migrate, but the Arctic tern travels furthest. The tern flies from the Arctic to the Antarctic. Then it flies back again. This makes a trip of 32,000 kilometres.

b Some animals can regrow parts of their bodies if they are damaged. For example, the starfish can grow new 'arms.' Starfish have five arms. Another example of this phenomenon is the slowworm. It can regrow a broken-off tail. Lizards can also grow new tails.

c The giant squid has the largest eyes of any animal. Its eyes can be 39cm across. This is 16 times wider than a human eye.

20 Which of the following would you probably find in a typical discursive essay?

a physical descriptions of people or places
b the writer's opinions
c arguments for or against an idea
d tables of statistics
e a sequence of events
f examples illustrating ideas

21 Add commas where necessary to these sentences.

a In my opinion digital technology is making the world a safer more pleasant place to live.

b During his long working life my grandfather was a policeman a farmer a gardener and a lorry driver.

c Anost which is in the Morran district of France has a music festival every year.

d Apples bananas and oranges are quite sweet. Lemons by contrast are sour.

e Although there's a speed limit of 60kph on this road many drivers go over 100kph.

22 Choose one of the following essay questions and write the opening and closing paragraphs of your answer.

a *'The best way to reduce the number of private cars on public roads is to charge motorists for every kilometre they drive.' What are your opinions?*

b *Children spend too long in compulsory education and should be allowed to leave school and start work at the age of 14. What are your views?*

----

23 Write five true sentences about the information in this chart.

Top five languages used on the Web
Number of internet users by language

Languages	% of all internet users	Internet users by language	World population estimate for the language
English	29.7%	322 million	1.125 billion
Chinese	13.3%	144 million	1.340 billion
Japanese	7.9%	86 million	128 million
Spanish	7.5%	81 million	437 million
German	5.4%	58 million	98 million

Appendix 1
Useful language

Unit 1

1.1 Asking for information

I would like to know whether …
Could you let us know …?
Can we pay by credit card / by cheque / in euros / in pounds?

1.2 Stating requirements / needs

I am looking for accommodation for four people for five nights in June.
These are our requirements: …
We need the following: …

1.3 Accommodation vocabulary

rooms: double room / single room
beds: double bed / single bed / twin beds / (baby's) cot
accommodation: full board / half board / bed and breakfast (B&B)
conference facilities / deposit / guest house / caravan / camper van

Unit 2

2.1 Conversational words and expressions.

Hi / Good thinking! / loads of trouble / hang out with / Great news! / Brilliant idea / Cheers

2.2 Shortened words and abbreviations

prob. / CU (see you) soon

2.3 Missing words

(It was) Good to hear from you.
(We're) Glad you had a good time.
(I) Hope you enjoy Libya. / (Do you) Remember?
(I) Suppose I shouldn't complain.
(I) Know what you mean.

2.4 Colloquial grammar.

There's several good restaurants. (There **are** …)
less phone calls (**fewer**)
They didn't used to go out. (didn't **use** to)

Unit 3

3.1 Types of information

- **Name**
  forename / first name / surname / family name / full name / maiden name (woman's name before marriage) / initials / Signature
- **Other personal information**
  Date of birth (DOB) / Age / Sex: M/F
- **Marital status**
  single / married / divorced / separated / widowed
- **Address**
  permanent / temporary / Home / Work / email
- **Numbers**
  Tel. No. / Bank Acc. No./ Passport No.

3.2 Instructions

- PLEASE USE BLACK INK AND BLOCK CAPITALS
- Please make sure you complete all questions relevant to you.
- If a question is not relevant, write N/A (not applicable).
- Remember to sign and date the form.
- Do not leave blank.

Unit 4

4.1 Starting

Dear Sir/Madam
I would like to draw your attention to …

4.2 Finishing

Yours faithfully,
Helen Bane (by email) / Tony Brown (London)

4.3 Other words and phrases

In response to your editorial,
In your newspaper (21 December)
As a regular reader, I …
Your readers may be interested to know that …

4.4 Qualifying opinions

My strong personal belief is …
I genuinely believe that …
I am quite sure that …
It's my considered opinion that …
The accepted view on this matter is …

4.5 Introductory adverbs which express an opinion

Astonishingly / Obviously / Interestingly

Unit**5**

5.1 Resolving a problem

To resolve this problem …
In order to resolve this unsatisfactory situation …
One way of dealing with this problem would be to …

5.2 Referring to something enclosed or attached

I am (now) enclosing/attaching …
Enclosed/Attached you will find …

5.3 Making a polite request

Could you possibly …?
Please could you …
I would be (most) grateful if you could …

5.4 Reminding someone of something they should know

As you may remember,
You will remember …
May I remind you (that) …

5.5 Referring to a previous contact

Further to our discussion, …
As (we) discussed earlier, …
With reference to our earlier (telephone) conversation, …
Regarding our recent discussion, …

Unit**6**

6.1 Abbreviations relevant to writing a CV

CV	curriculum vitae
DOB	date of birth
BA/BSc	Bachelor of Arts / Sciences
Econ	economics
Hons	honours (degree)
Adv.	advanced
SE (Asia)	South East
Dr	doctor
IT	Information Technology
IELTS	International English Language Testing System

Unit**7**

7.1 Job reference vocabulary

attitude	colleague	competence
confidential	current position	employee
employer	experience	in confidence
performance	qualifications	team working
(job) reference		

7.2 Personal qualities

dependable	enthusiastic	flexibility (n)
good-natured	honest	leadership (n)
polite / reliable / respectful		

7.3 Formal relative clauses

He is a person <u>for whom</u> I have great respect.
This is the address <u>to which</u> I sent the letter.
We're going on a journey, the start <u>of which</u> is the North Pole.

Unit**8**

8.1 Formal verb–noun collocations

to carry out a survey / to take part in a survey
to judge something by certain criteria
to score points / to award points
to give a grade
to analyse results

8.2 Other formal report language

to rate	a league table
overall result	the maximum possible grade
standard of service	to comment favourably

Unit**9**

9.1 Vocabulary related to technological products

everyday use	heavy-duty use
key features	model
pros and cons	satellite navigation
system	suitability
(not) suitable for …	user-friendly

Unit**10**

10.1 Vocabulary related to email

junk email / spam
receive an email
send an email

10.2 Using abbreviations

etc. / viz. / e.g.

10.3 Acronyms

BTW = *by the way*
FYI = *for your information*

Unit**11**

11.1 Selling yourself

I have a variety/range of experience of (*-ing*)
I have undertaken voluntary work
My first degree course, which was a BA in Philosophy, …
In addition to my academic study, I have a number of interests, …
When I was working on a summer play scheme, I took responsibility for …
The content of my course will assist me in (*-ing*)

11.2 Educational vocabulary

academic study   qualifications
a first degree   exam results
undergraduate   postgraduate course
to apply for a course   to specialize in a subject

11.3 Qualifications

BA   Bachelor of Arts
BSc   Bachelor of Science
MA   Master of Arts
MBA   Master of Business Administration
PhD   Doctor of Philosophy

11.4 Conjunctions

I'm planning to live and work in Beijing **when** I finish my course.
If I can afford it, I'll rent a flat in the city centre.
I'd prefer to live in the city **because** I'll be able to walk to work.
Although the rents are higher, I won't have to spend money on rail fares.
Going by rail takes time and money, **whereas** walking to work is cheap and healthy.
As I haven't finished my course yet, I can't make any real plans.

Notes
1 The clause which starts with the conjunction can be the first or the second part of a sentence.
2 If the clause which starts with the conjunction is first, it is separated from the second half of the sentence by a comma.

Unit 12

12.1 Symbols

∴ = therefore
∵ = because
≠ = does not equal
/ = or (for example red/blue = red or blue)
& or + = and/plus
≃ = approximately

12.2 Abbreviations

e.g. = for example   i.e. = that is
etc. = and so on   cf. = compare
viz. = namely   c. = about/approximately
NB = important note   imp. = important
max. = maximum   min. = minimum
Q = question   A = answer
ref. = reference   v. = very
s/t or stg = something   s/o = someone
sby = somebody

Unit 14

14.1 Pronouns

Archaeologists found the evidence **they** were looking for when someone gave **them** an old manuscript. The person **who** gave **it** to **them** went missing the next day.

14.2 Other reference words and phrases

6 June and 16 December were my parents' birthdays. I'll never forget **these dates**.
You're going to London on Tuesday? I'll be **there** myself **then**.

Unit 15

15.1 Expressing personal opinions

In my opinion/view,   It is my opinion/view that …
I would say that …
I (strongly) believe that …
It is my (firm) belief that …
It is a commonly held view that …

15.2 Introducing an example to back up an argument

for instance/example   To take an example,

15.3 Talking about possibilities

(tensions) **may** arise if …   this **can** cause (stress)
there's **a possibility** that … it is **possible** that …

15.4 Concluding the essay

In conclusion, …   To conclude, …

Unit 16

16.1 Words and expressions referring to trends and movements

a huge rise
a sharp drop
a slight increase
to rise / to increase
to fall / to drop / to decrease

16.2 Words and expressions used to compare

In comparison with …
Compared to …
This compares to …

Appendix 2
Text types and styles

The terms *formal*, *informal* and *neutral* used to describe the style appropriate to the text types listed below are generalizations, not authoritative classifications. The range of styles available to a writer is a continuum from *ultra-formal*, which is essential in a legal document, to *conversational*, which is perfectly acceptable in an email or in a text message. Exactly where on this style continuum a particular piece of writing fits depends on a number of factors:
- the reader: who they are, how well you know them and what style they expect
- the purpose of writing
- the conventions associated with the text type.

This is why a choice of styles is sometimes suggested in this list. If you are not sure what style to use and do not know the reader particularly well, it is advisable to use a formal or neutral style.

Please note that the Formal/informal/neutral column in the table below describes the text which appears in this book. You may find examples elsewhere where other levels of formality are used for these types of writitng.

Text type	Formal / informal / neutral	Unit
Letters / emails		
– Asking about accommodation	formal	U1
– Keeping in touch with friends	informal	U2
– Replying to emails	informal	U2
– Expressing opinions	formal	U4
– Complaining about faulty goods / services	formal	U5
– Covering letter to accompany CV	formal	U6
– Emails in a work context	formal / informal / neutral	U10
Filling in forms		
– Online accommodation booking	formal	U1
– Visa application form	formal	U3
– Delayed flight departure claim form	formal	U3
– Personal effects claim form	formal	U3
– Curriculum vitae form	formal	U6
– Job reference form	formal	U7
Curriculum vitae / Résumé	formal	U6
Job references	formal	U7
Personal statement related to education course	formal	U11
Reports		
– Report based on a customer survey	neutral	U8
– Report based on statistics presented in tables or graphic form	neutral	U16
Notes		
– Notes for a product presentation	informal / neutral	U9
– Notes on a lecture or talk	informal / neutral	U12
– Notes for giving a seminar	neutral	U13
– Handout to accompany seminar	formal / neutral	U13
Summary	formal / neutral	U14
Essay	formal	U15

Formal (polite, distant, indirect)	Neutral (semi-formal – when style is not an issue)	Informal (friendly, personal, casual, direct)
Agreeing I would (completely) agree that …	I agree. I think you're right.	You're right (there). That's true. / True.
Disagreeing I can't/couldn't (possibly) agree (that) …	I don't agree (that) …	You're wrong (there). / That's not true. Nonsense! / Rubbish!
Apologizing Please accept my (sincere) apologies (for + -ing)	I am very sorry about	I'm (really) sorry. / Sorry (about …)
Asking for advice I would (really) appreciate your advice about … Could I ask for your advice about …?	Can I ask your advice about …? What would you advise me to do about …?	What should / shall I do about …?
Giving advice My advice would be to … I would advise you to … If I were in your position, I would …	I think you ought to … It might be an idea to … If I were you, I'd …	(I think) You should … Why don't you …? I'd …
Asking for permission With your permission, I should like to … May I have (your) permission to …?	Would it be possible for me to …? Could I (possibly) …? Would you mind if I …?	Can I …? Is it okay / all right if I …?
Commenting on an idea I think that's an excellent idea.	That's a very good idea.	Brilliant! / Great idea!
Commiserating I do sympathize.	I'm sorry to hear that.	Sorry about …
Complaining I wish to complain about … This is most unsatisfactory / disappointing.	This is not good enough. What are you going to do about …?	I've had enough (of this).
Congratulating Please accept my congratulations.	Congratulations!	Well done!
Giving an example One / An example of this would be …	Take … as an example.	For example, … / For instance, …
Opinions I believe that … My personal belief is that … It is my considered opinion / view that … It would seem to me that …	It's my opinion that … In my opinion, … I would say that … It's possible that … It seems to me that …	I think … / What I think is … I'd say that …
Reminding someone about something As you may / will remember, … May / Could I remind you that …?	Do you remember …? You haven't forgotten …, have you?	Do you / D'you remember …?

Formal (polite, distant, indirect)	Neutral (semi-formal – when style is not an issue)	Informal (friendly, personal, casual, direct)
Requests Please could you let me know whether … I would be (most / very) grateful if you could … Could you possibly explain how …?	I'd like to know whether … Could you …?	Do you / D'you know if …? Can you tell me if …? What I'd like to know is …
Saying you are pleased I was pleased to hear that …	I'm glad to hear …	Glad to hear … / Pleased to know … Great news!
Saying what you are interested in My interests include … I have always been interested in …	I'm really interested in … I have many interests, including … My main interest is …	I'm really keen on … I'm really into …
Starting letters / emails Dear Mr / Mrs / Ms /Miss / X, **Ending letters** Yours faithfully, / Yours sincerely,	Dear Mr X, / John, Best wishes, / Regards,	Hi (John), / John See you, / Cheers, / Tom (*writer's name only*)
Stating requirements / needs We require accommodation on + date … We require the following …	We are looking for a room on + date … These are our requirements: …	We need a room on + date … This is what we need: …
Surprise I was very / most surprised to hear that … I find it astonishing that …	I was really surprised about …	What a surprise! I don't believe it!
Thanking Thank you very much for your letter … Thank you, I'm most grateful.	Thank you for your letter / email …	Thanks / Thanks a lot for the letter / email.

Appendix 4
Spelling

Introductory note

English spelling is notoriously tricky. This is because words are not always spelt the way they sound. In fact there are often several different ways of spelling the same sound. Then there is the added complication of the differences between British and American spelling. (Remember if you use a computer spell-checker you should choose US or UK English. However, also remember that a computer spellchecker only checks that words are spelt correctly, not used in the correct context, e.g. it cannot differentiate between *their* and *there*.) Below are some notes to help you. Although they are not exhaustive, use them to help you focus on common errors to look out for in your essays.

Helpful rules or patterns of spelling

Error	Correction	Notes / explanation
helpfull / carefull	helpful / careful **but** helpfully / carefully	The adjective *full* meaning not empty ends in double *ll*, but as a suffix added to adjectives there is only one *-l*. However, the adverb formed from the adjective ends in double *ll*.
magicly / phoneticly	magically / phonetically	Adverbs formed from adjectives ending in *–ic*, end in *–ically*. Exception: *publicly*
stoping / weter	stopping / wetter **but** beating / longer	The final consonant of some words is doubled before an ending is added. This only happens to words which end in one short vowel and one consonant.
targetting / benefitting	targeting / benefiting **but** travelling / marvellous	If the stress is on the first syllable of a word with two or more syllables, the final consonant does not double. In British English, this rule does not apply to words ending in *–l*.
recieve / cieling	receive / ceiling	The usual combination of letters making this sound is *–ie*, but after the letter *c*, it is normally *–ei*. Exception: *seize*
english / dutch	English / Dutch	Nationality adjectives begin with a capital letter, as if they were proper nouns.
potatos / heros	potatoes / heroes	Most nouns which end in *–o* in the singular, add *–es* to form the plural. Exceptions: *radios / pianos / kilos / videos*
ladys / babys monkies / trollies	ladies / babies **but** monkeys / trolleys	The plural of nouns ending in a consonant + *y* is *–ies*. If there is a vowel before the final *y*, form the plural by adding *–s*.
lable / towle	label / towel	Most nouns which end in the sound 'bl', are spelt *–le*, for example: *bottle, table, battle, single, double*. But there are some that end in *–el*, for example: *parcel / angel*.
cuver / luve	cover / love	In English there are no words with the combination of letters *uv* (pronounced /ʌv/).
allthough / allmost	although / almost	Some words in English starting with the sound *all* start *al-* *almighty / altogether / although / also / almost / already / always / alright*
paniced / trafficing	panicked / trafficking	Verbs which end in *–c*, add the letter *–k* before an ending.
docter / directer	doctor / director	Most words for people who do things in English end in *–er*. Most of the words that end in *–or*, have the letters *-ct* or *–t* before the ending. Exceptions: *tailor / sailor / donor / survivor* A few other words end in *–ar* *beggar / burglar / liar*

Homophones

There are many sets of homophones in English. Homophones are words which sound the same, but have different meanings and are spelt differently. Confusion between these sets of words often leads to spelling errors. Here are some of the most common .

Homophones	Meanings
four for	number – *one, two, three, **four** …* preposition – *This present is **for** you.*
their there	possessive adjective – *This is **their** car.* adverb – *I'd hate to live **there**.*
two too to	number – *She has **two** brothers.* adverb – more than is necessary. *That coat's **too** big for me.* preposition – *I'm going **to** bed.*
sale sail	noun – occasion when things are sold: *A book **sale**.* verb – travel on water: *We'll **sail** across the Mediterranean.*
site sight cite	noun – place: *We visited an ancient burial **site**.* noun – ability to see: *I need my **sight** testing.* verb – to refer to / quote: *They **cite** the two main causes of crime.*
weigh way	verb – check how heavy something is: *I **weigh** myself regularly.* noun – road / route / method: *Can you tell me the **way** to the station?*
whether weather	conjunction like *if* – *I asked him **whether** he was hungry.* noun – *The **weather's** been terrible this week.*
principle principal	noun – belief/moral: *He behaves badly. He has no **principles**.* adjective – main: *What's your **principal** reason for wanting this job?* noun – director: *Our college has a new **principal**.*
court caught	noun – Place where trials are held: *They took him to **court**.* past participle of *catch* – *I think I may have **caught** your cold.*
whole hole	adjective – entire: *I've spent the **whole** day relaxing.* noun – empty space: *I've got a **hole** in my pocket.*
meet meat	verb – *Let's **meet** outside the cinema at midday, shall we?* noun – *I don't eat **meat**. I'm a vegetarian.*

Other commonly misspelt words

accommodate / accommodation
calendar
conscientious
conscious
definitely
embarrassment / embarrassing
existence
grammar
harass
hierarchy

indispensable
inoculate
millennium
miniature
minuscule
mischievous
misspell
noticeable
occurrence / occurred / occurring
pastime

perseverance
precede / preceding
privilege
questionnaire
rhythm
separate / separately
supersede
weird
withhold

Punctuation marks and examples	Rule
Full stop . Some people know nothing about punctuation. Try and relax the night before exams, e.g. listen to music, cook a meal etc.	Use full stops … – at the end of a sentence – between letters of some abbreviations
Comma , I like apples, bananas, cherries and oranges. When you've finished, can you give me a hand? Children, however, are allowed in free. Amazingly, he wasn't injured in the accident. My son, who is a teacher, lives in Indonesia.	Use commas … – between items on a list – after a subordinate clause at the beginning of a sentence – before and after words or phrases which interrupt a sentence – after an adverb (phrase) at the beginning of a sentence – before (or before and after) a non-defining relative clause
Apostrophe ' This is my father's study. This is my parents' bedroom. You shouldn't make promises you can't keep.	Use apostrophes … – to show possession or ownership – to show that letters have been left out
Colon : This is what we need: food, water and blankets. I've never liked sailing: it makes me feel sick.	Use colons … – to introduce a list – to introduce more details or an explanation
Semi-colon ; I've never enjoyed flying; in fact, I actually hate it. There are three reasons for this: it makes me feel physically ill; I prefer to travel more slowly; the seats are always too small.	Use semi-colons … – instead of a full stop, where the meaning of two ideas is very close – between items on a list, especially where items are long or not simple grammatically
Dash – That was the best thing about our holiday – we all managed to relax. I've got three complaints – the weather, the food and the hotel. The hotel – which was only half-built – cost a fortune.	Use dashes … in informal writing instead of commas, colons and semi-colons
Question mark ? Do you know when to use a question mark? He asked me whether he should use a question mark in a reported question.	Use question marks – at the end of a direct question, – **but not** at the end of an indirect or reported question
Speech / Quotation marks "…" The first thing he said was, "You've lost weight." I've never understood the word "bland". Have you ever read 'The Old Man and the Sea'?	Use speech marks … – to quote direct speech – around words we want to draw particular attention to. – single quotation marks for the names of books, films, etc.
Capital letters The most romantic city in the world is Paris, the capital of France. The assassination of President Kennedy took place in Dallas in 1963. There have been 42 presidents of the US. My birthday was on Thursday 17 May. The man I was talking to … …was Russian.	Use capital letters – to start a sentence – for the names of places and people – for people's titles **but not** for jobs – for abbreviations or acronyms – for days and months – for the 1st person pronoun "I" – for nationality adjectives

Appendix 6
Editing your writing

Writing accurate English is an important part of knowing the language, especially if you are taking written exams, or you need to use English in your work.

In general, when working through the writing tasks in this book, we suggest that you write two drafts:
– The purpose of the first draft is mainly to set down information, ideas or opinions within an appropriate structure.
– The purpose of the second or final draft should be to edit the first draft, to check your style, grammar, spelling and punctuation.

If you are working in a class, you can exchange writing with another student and edit each other's first drafts.

Here are some of the points to think about as you edit your writing:

Style

– What is the purpose of your writing? Is a particular style appropriate for this type of writing?
– Who will read your writing? Will readers expect a certain layout or level of formality? (For example, a potential employer would expect to receive a formal letter, with paragraphs, with your CV.)
– If your writing is intended to be formal, check that you have not used any verb contractions or slang expressions, and that you have not omitted necessary words.

Structure

– Is the structure of your writing appropriate to the type of text? For example, if you are writing an academic essay, have you included an introduction and a conclusion?
– Have you started a new paragraph for each new idea? Is the new idea clearly expressed in a topic sentence?

Grammar

– Have you used the correct form of appropriate verb tenses?
– Do the subject and verb in each sentence agree?
– Have you used the correct word order, for example in questions, indirect questions, and sentences which begin with negative expressions?
– Have you used the correct prepositions after verbs and adjectives?
– Have you used articles appropriately?

Spelling

– Have you thought carefully about the spelling of words you know are difficult – for example, homophones and words which you personally find tricky.
– If you are using a computer spellchecker, have you set it to the correct language: British or American English?
– If you are using a dictionary, have you chosen the word which expresses your intended idea?

Vocabulary

– Have you used correct or appropriate collocations? (e.g. *make* a mistake; *absolutely* terrifying)
– Have you used formal or informal vocabulary consistently?

Punctuation

– Check your use of the following punctuation marks: full stops, commas, colons, semi-colons, apostrophes and dashes.
– Have you used capital letters for all proper nouns, nationality adjectives, the first words of sentences and for the first person pronoun *I*?

Other points

– Have you used prepositions, reference words, synonyms and other devices to avoid repetition?

Audioscript

These recordings are mostly in standard British English. Where a speaker has a different accent, it is added in brackets. The recording numbers below match the track numbers on the audio CD.

Unit2

Machine Please leave a message after the beep.

Mum Hello, John – this is Mum. I've just been shopping in town and bumped into your old friend Charlie. He's here for a week visiting his parents. He asked me to give you his email address so that you could contact him about meeting up while he's around. I said I was sure you'd like to see him. Anyway, his email is charlie56@ hotmail.org. Call me when you can. Bye, darling.

Review1

Caroline Hello. Central Bank complaints department. My name's Caroline. How can I help?

Ms O'Brien Hello. I'd like to follow up a complaint I made over a month ago, regarding a direct debit.

Caroline Could I take some details first, please? Could you tell me your name?

Ms O'Brien Yes, it's Helen O'Brien.

Caroline Is that Ms or Mrs?

Ms O'Brien Ms.

Caroline Thank you. And your address?

Ms O'Brien It's 27, The Avenue, Potters Bar, Hertfordshire.

Caroline Thank you – and the postcode?

Ms O'Brien It's EN6 4HN.

Caroline And your phone number?

Ms O'Brien 01707 888163.

Caroline And finally your bank account number?

Ms O'Brien 22 76 93 54.

Caroline 22 67 83 54.

Ms O'Brien No, 76 93.

Caroline Sorry. And when did you first contact us with this problem?

Ms O'Brien It was on June the 16th this year.

Caroline June 16th. Can you tell me briefly what the problem is?

Ms O'Brien Yes. It goes back to May – the sixteenth of May to be exact. I phoned my local branch to ask them to cancel a direct debit payment to my electricity supplier. The money was normally taken from my account on the 15th day of each month.

Caroline And when did you realize there was a problem?

Ms O'Brien On the 15th of June when the electricity company took money out of my account – as usual.

Caroline In other words, the direct debit payments had not been stopped by us?

Ms O'Brien Correct. I rang immediately and was assured this would not happen again. We're now in July and it has just happened. The normal payment has gone from the account again.

Caroline I see. Do you know who you spoke to at the bank on either of the occasions when you rang?

Ms O'Brien No, I'm afraid not. But someone isn't doing their job properly.

Caroline I quite agree. All I can do is to apologize on behalf of the bank. I will report this to my manager and someone will phone you back later in the day.

Ms O'Brien Thank you. I shall expect to hear from someone later today, then.

Caroline Thank you, Ms O'Brien. Goodbye.

Unit9

(Presenter = American)

Presenter The ability to jump two metres in the air may not be something you've thought too much about. And being able to run at 30 kilometres an hour most people have never considered. But just stop for a moment and think about how our new product could change your life. One obvious use would be getting to work. Unless you work from home, your daily journey to your place of work is probably a mad dash for the train or the bus. There's no point in taking your car because there are traffic jams every morning, and anyway the car parks are probably very expensive or, worse still, full. Here's where Powerizers can help. It takes just a couple of minutes to strap them on and you're away, overtaking your pedestrian neighbours or even leaping over obstacles that might slow you down.

That's the practical, everyday use for our product, but then there's sport and exercise. According to industry experts, Powerizers are set to be the next extreme sport, and the ultimate keep-fit gadget. They've been on the market for less than a year, but already there are over fifty Powerizers clubs in this country, and plans are being made for a Powerizers Olympics in the near future. Imagine the 100 metres, the high jump or basketball performed by athletes wearing Powerizers. And what better way to tone up your muscles and keep fit? When they catch on, Powerizers are expected to put many traditional gyms out of business!

From a technical angle, our product is very simple. It is powered by a superlight spring, which harnesses the gravitational pull from your body weight and propels you to superhuman feats. Powerizers come in a range of sizes to suit men and women of all heights and weights, although we do not recommend that Powerizers be used by children under the age of 12.

To date there have been no recorded cases of serious injury related to the use of Powerizers, but extreme caution is recommended until users are completely familiar with our product. We strongly advise the wearing of protective clothing, including knee and elbow pads and a helmet.

According to one experienced user we interviewed, Powerizers make you feel as if you're walking on the moon. Movements forwards and upwards are almost effortless. So that's about all, except of course for the price. We make two different models of Powerizers: Basic and Professional. The Basic model is designed for the occasional user and costs around $500. The Professional model, which is designed for competitive use, has a more substantial structure and different springs, though that comes at the increased price of $800.

5

(Presenter = Australian)

Presenter Many people prefer their music from on-ear rather than in-ear headphones, but they don't want to hear all those outside noises that so often interfere with their listening pleasure. If you're one of those people, you will benefit from our SoftRelax noise-blocking headphones. Over the past 5 years, our engineers have developed new technologies which eliminate 90% of unwanted intrusive sounds and allow you to listen to the sounds you want to hear. Whether this is Mozart, the latest chart hits or your favourite spoken word radio programmes, SoftRelax headphones' crystal-clear audio enables you to hear recordings as they were made – full of power and subtlety.

They're ideal for wearing if you're travelling – especially by air or rail. The noise-blocking mechanism copes easily with the roar of aircraft or train engines. Believe it or not, you can actually think. They're equally useful in the office or the home, where you may want to shut out the noise. No headphones will block all outside noises, but our SoftRelax headphones will improve almost any listening experience.

If you thought all on-ear headphones were big and clumsy to wear, take a close look at our product. We guarantee that you can wear them for hours at a time, with no discomfort. They are lightweight and compact and come in a light protective bag that will fit easily into a pocket or briefcase. Each set of headphones is supplied with two rechargeable batteries and a battery charger kit, as well as a variety of cables to allow you to pair them with a range of sound sources, from your mobile phone to your laptop.

We can't pretend that our headphones are cheap, but we can claim that they are the best on the market. There are two models: the Home model and the Studio model, which is for heavy-duty use, for example by sound engineers in recording studios. The Home model costs £250 and the Studio model is £320.

SoftRelax headphones are guaranteed for five years and will be replaced without question if they fail during that period. That's how confident we are.

Unit 10

6

X Hello?

Kate Hi, it's Kate

X Hi Kate. How's things?

Kate Fine. Look, I haven't much time, I need to ask a favour.

X Okay.

Kate Could you email Ed and tell him I've missed my train and I won't be there until about 12 o'clock? I've tried phoning him myself, but he's not at his desk.

X Okay. Is that all?

Kate No, I'm afraid not. I was supposed to be having a meeting with Ed at 9.30. We were going to discuss the details of flexitime working in time for Ed to talk to all the office staff at 11 o'clock.

X Okay – what do you want me to tell him?

Kate Well, firstly, as far as I'm concerned, flexitime working is an excellent idea, especially for those employees who have young children. We can't open it only to those people, so we have to give everyone an opportunity of working flexible hours.

X Is that it?

Kate No. Can you also say that I think flexitime should not be completely flexible? I mean, there's no point in people working between 8 o'clock at night and 4 o'clock in the morning when there's hardly anyone else around. So I think we should say everyone should work for an eight-hour period between 7 in the morning and 8 at night.

X Okay – between 7 and 8.

Kate Yeah. That's it.

X I think I've got that. I'll do it straight away.

Kate Thanks – oh, and tell Ed I'm sorry. I'll be there as soon as I can.

X Will do. Bye Kate.

Unit 11

7

Extract 1

(Speaker = American)

You've probably been working long enough to feel the social and technological changes which are affecting the world of business. Do you sometimes wonder whether you have the know-how to keep up with the pace of change? If your answer to this question is 'Yes', maybe you should consider enrolling on our 15-month Masters in Business Administration programme. Our wide-ranging curriculum will prepare you for business leadership in the 21st century. Our 13-week foundation course introduces key business areas and leads into a 12-

month intensive program which includes lectures and seminars designed to address course members' individual needs. In addition to this, the course includes guest speakers, site visits and practical case studies. In the final stages of the course, we offer personalized career management advice and training to help you find the position you're looking for.

Extract 2

Our American Studies course is an inter-disciplinary degree programme offering you the chance to study the politics, history, literature, cinema and popular culture of the United States. The first year, which is taught mainly by lectures and tutorials, provides an introduction to America and its people, as well as some of the key political and social issues which have dominated the USA during the last hundred years. In the second year, students have the opportunity to study at the University of California, one of our partner institutions. In the final year, students produce a dissertation and choose 4 units from a list of options, ranging from 20th century American Art to Black American Writing and the History of Hollywood.

Unit 12

8 (Presenter = Indian)

Presenter My talk this morning is about a subject dear to all our hearts: happiness. I shall be trying to identify some of the factors that make for a happy life. Believe it or not, scientists have been studying this subject in recent years and have come up with some very interesting results. In my talk, I shall be considering eight of the factors which may or may not affect people's happiness.

Let's start with the relationship between money and happiness. Can money buy happiness? The short answer is, yes – but it doesn't buy you very much. Researchers have found that, on average, wealthier people are happier. Of course, there are rich people who are miserable and poor people who are happy, but if you're an unhappy rich person, you're probably happier than if you are an unhappy poor person. But the link between money and happiness is a bit more complex than that. In recent years, average income has skyrocketed in industrialized countries, yet happiness levels have remained static. The key seems to be whether or not you have more money than your friends, neighbours and colleagues. Human beings seem more concerned with comparative status than with absolute wealth.

Let's move on to the question of 'desire'. Throughout history, wise people have pointed out that limiting your desires is a surer route to happiness than a fat bank balance – and they may be right. In the 1980s, researchers asked college students in 39 countries to rate their happiness. Then they asked them how close they were to having all they wanted in life. They found that the people whose aspirations – not just for money, but for friends, family, job, health and money – were a long way beyond what they already had, tended to be less happy than those who perceived a smaller gap.

9 (Presenter = Indian)

Presenter Okay, thirdly, there's no connection between intelligence and happiness. This may seem surprising, since brighter people tend to earn more money and richer people tend to be happier. Some researchers think there must be some other factor ruining the lives of smarter people, but so far they have only been able to speculate about what it is. One idea is that brighter people may have higher expectations and so be more dissatisfied. The next question scientists asked was 'Are some people born happier than others?' Psychologists believe that our feeling of well-being is determined partly by what is happening in our lives, and partly by a personal happiness level, which is up to 90% genetically determined. Studies have shown, however, that personality and happiness are linked. So, for example, extroverts tend to be a lot happier than introverts. This could be because extroverts are more likely to do things that bring happiness, such as have friends, climb the job ladder and get married.

The fifth factor relates to physical appearance. First the bad news: good-looking people really are happier. Perhaps the explanation for this is that life is kinder to the beautiful. Or it could be more subtle than that. The most attractive faces are highly symmetrical, and there is evidence from animal research that symmetry reflects good genes and a healthy immune system. So perhaps beautiful people are happier because they are healthier. The real secret is to believe you look great. Unfortunately, this is harder than it sounds. Most people have a distorted self-image that tends to be negative.

10 (Presenter = Indian)

Presenter Okay, moving on to point 6, reports from 42 countries show that married people are consistently happier than single people. We do not yet know for certain whether marriage makes you happy, or whether happy people are more likely to get married. Both may be true. In a study that followed more than 30,000 Germans for 15 years, it was found that happy people are more likely to get married and stay married.

Point seven – being kind to other people may also make people happier. Several studies have found a link between happiness and altruistic behaviour. But as with many behavioural traits, it is not always clear whether doing good makes you feel good, or whether happy people are more likely to be altruistic. In a study of 3,617 people, it was found that happy people were more likely to take on voluntary work. But they also found that volunteers became happier, and the more voluntary work they did, the happier they were. And finally, old age may not be as bad as people presume. Elderly people are on average just as happy as the young, and actually rate themselves more satisfied with their lives overall. In a study of 2,727 people aged between 25 and 74, researchers found that other things such as gender, personality type and social factors affect how you feel as you get older. For instance, both men and women tended to experience more positive emotions as they aged. Why are old people so happy? Some researchers suggest that they're more realistic about their goals, only setting ones that they know they can achieve.

Well that's it for today. Next week, we'll be looking in more detail at how age affects people's self-image and sense of worth.

11 (Ana = Spanish)

Ana Today we're going to look at what we mean by social status. In simple terms, sociologists define the term as the prestige attached to a person's position in society. What is particularly interesting, of course, is how we decide who has high status and who has low status in society.

The first point to make is that in modern societies, a person's job is usually thought of as the main determinant of their status.

Having said that, other factors can also have an important influence, for example: ethnic background, gender, religion and education. In the past, in some societies a person's social status could depend on which particular class that person happened to have been born into, or whether the person was born male or female. In certain situations today, for example a British secondary school, status may depend on the clothes a student wears or on the style of their hair. In some societies family relationships are the basis of status; for example, in certain parts of Africa a man's mother-in-law has a higher status than her son-in-law.

Status may depend upon inherited characteristics such as gender, or upon characteristics that individuals have gained through their own efforts, like educational qualifications. But whatever it is based on, social status is, and has been a feature of all societies throughout history.

Unit 13

12

Jonathan Good morning, my name's Jonathan May, and in this morning's presentation I am going to look at a trend in advertising that has become apparent during the last three or four years in a number of western countries. The trend I am referring to is the changing images of men and women in television commercials, and my aim is to examine why so many advertisers have adopted these images. Let's start by thinking about two current TV commercials that have become famous, or perhaps infamous, with the general public. There's the one featuring a young man who takes a new girlfriend back to his flat, then pretends he's been burgled as an explanation for why his flat is so untidy. He tells the girl he's going to report the burglary to the police, but secretly phones an emergency cleaning service to come and tidy the flat. We find the idea funny, but not surprising, because the young man is a recognizable stereotype: a lazy, messy, dishonest slob!

Then there's the particularly nasty commercial for a car in which a man has fallen out of his second floor window and is dangling by his fingertips high above the ground. Luckily, when he falls, he will

land on a car, and probably be only slightly hurt. A woman sees the unfortunate man and tells him to hang on. But, instead of helping him, she gets into the car and drives away. The message is clear: the car is so precious to this selfish woman that she'll do anything to stop it being damaged, even though this may mean that the dangling man is seriously injured. According to the Advertising Control Authority, complaints from men about the way they are depicted in TV commercials have increased ten times in the last five years. It seems that what men once regarded as inoffensive or even funny can now cause serious and widespread offence. In another survey, carried out by a well-respected marketing organization, it was found that of more than a thousand adults questioned, two thirds said women in ads appeared generally caring and intelligent, but were sometimes assertive to the point of aggression or even cruelty. By contrast, most men were generally depicted as weak, lazy and incompetent. So what is the advertisers' motivation in portraying men and women in this way? Surely not just to amuse television viewers. No, the most likely explanation, according to advertising industry experts, is that by empowering women at the expense of men, advertisers hope to appeal to women. However, while there is some evidence that this strategy worked in the beginning, it now seems probable that it's having a negative impact. By provoking sympathy for the men in their commercials, advertisers may actually be putting women off buying their products. Women, it seems, do not like being portrayed as cruel manipulators of men. So what can we conclude from this investigation? The message to advertisers seems obvious and straightforward: if you want women to buy your products, flatter women, but don't insult and denigrate men in the process. Maybe more women would have bought the car in the commercial I referred to at the beginning of my presentation if the woman had helped to save the desperate man by letting him fall on to the roof of her car. The commercial could have ended with a shot of an undamaged car roof!
Thank you very much. Now, are there any questions? Yes, …

Unit 15

 13

Radio presenter In tonight's programme we look at an issue that's rarely out of the news these days: climate change. Most commentators believe that climate change is brought about by increases in average temperature across the world. Almost every day, there are dire warnings from experts that unless something is done immediately, it will be impossible to prevent a global catastrophe which will change life on Earth forever. They say that we must all change our lifestyle now. But for every doom-monger, there is a sceptic who claims that climate change is the result of natural processes and not human activity, and that nothing governments or individuals can do will affect the speed of change.
In the face of two convincing sets of arguments, what are we, the general public, to think? How should we react to these warnings? In this programme experts on both sides of the debate put their point of view. In the second part of the programme, listeners will have a chance to ask questions and challenge the experts' views.
Let's start with the argument which says that climate change is caused by human activity …

Review 2

 14

(Speaker = American)
Driving to work is one the main causes of environmental pollution, gridlocked towns and cities, and an unfit population.
If you ask people why they don't travel to work on public transport, the answer they often give is something like this: 'I live five kilometres from the nearest station,' or: 'The bus doesn't stop anywhere near my office.' The solution for these people couldn't be easier. What they need is a fold-up bike that is light enough to be carried easily by one person on a busy bus or train.
Our Bike-U-Fold can be folded up or unfolded in less than ten seconds and is available in men's and women's models. It is suitable for anyone over the age of 12 who can ride a bike. The price of both models is $99.

 15

We all know saving money is one of the most basic concepts of personal financial planning, and frequently the key to financial success. Yet many of us don't have a formal savings plan. Without such a plan, the chances of ever saving enough money to meet long-term financial goals or achieve financial security are pretty slim.
It seems simple, doesn't it? In order to save money, you need to have 'extra' cash, right? This is a common misconception. Having a spending plan, or 'budget', will help you create money for savings. Most of us, by setting spending goals, can manage to save regularly, so if you're tempted to forget the whole idea because you simply don't have enough money to have a formal savings plan, STOP! I'm going to let you into some of the 'secrets' of successful saving.
First of all, set yourself a few short-term and long-term financial goals to work towards, like a down payment on a car or home. Include the amount of money you need and a time frame for achieving your goal. It's much more motivating to save when you know what you're saving for. And remember, a goal that isn't written down is only a dream.

Answerkey

Get ready to write

- *Your own answers. Possible answers*:
  Positive adjectives: comfortable; convenient; elegant; friendly; homely; luxurious; sophisticated; value for money; well-equipped; well-run
  Negative adjectives: badly-equipped; badly-run; basic; dirty; inconvenient; out-of-the-way; overpriced; remote; scruffy; uncomfortable; unfriendly
- *Your own answer.*
- *Your own answer.*
- *Your own answer.*
- *Your own answer. Possible answer*:
  I would look on the Internet or in a guidebook, or I might ask a friend or person I know who has visited the same area.

1 a Extract 1: Hotel (four double rooms and two single rooms)
   Extract 2: Cottage (a double room, a room with twin beds and a single room for a disabled man)
  b Extract 1: A group of colleagues: ten adults
   Extract 2: A family: two adults, two children, a baby and a disabled elderly man
  c Extract 1: conference facilities: a meeting room with a projector, screen, internet access, etc.
   Extract 2: a cot, a downstairs bedroom, wheelchair access from the driveway.

2 a Extract 1 is a normal email from a home computer, while Extract 2 is a booking form from a website which can be completed online and sent, as an email, directly to the holiday agent.
   In Extract 1, the writer has decided the content and structure of what he/she writes. In Extract 2, what is written is determined by the structure and layout of the online form.
   In both emails, the writers mention special requirements. In Extract 1, the group needs a meeting room; in Extract 2, the writer mentions the needs of a baby and a disabled person.
  b *credit card* – if you pay by credit card, the money does not leave your account for several days or weeks. You may have to pay interest on money you borrow for more than a few weeks.
   debit card – if you pay by debit card, the money leaves a bank account immediately.
   cheque –if you pay by cheque, the person you pay puts the cheque into their bank account and the money leaves your account several days later.
   bank transfer – if you pay by bank transfer, the money is paid directly from your bank account to the account of the person you are paying.
  c *full board* is breakfast, lunch, evening meal and bed. Hotels also offer *half board*, which is breakfast, evening meal and bed, and *bed and breakfast*, which is what it says. Some hotels also offer bed only.

3 *Your own answers.*

Focus on If so,… / If not…

Your own answers. Possible answers:
a If so, could you send me a menu, please? If not, we may have to choose another hotel.
b If so, how much do they cost? If not, would it be possible to have a child's room next to an adult room?
c If so, is access free or is there a charge? If not, could you tell me whether there is an internet café nearby?

4 *Your own answer. Possible answer*:
  Hello,
  I have just found your website and would like to make a few enquiries about your hotel and its facilities.
  I am looking for accommodation for a group of six post-graduate students. The purpose for our stay is mainly to have a relaxing break, but we will also be doing some planning for a university business studies project. We require three rooms with twin beds for three nights, 16–18 April. We would require bed, breakfast and evening meal.
  I should explain that one of our group is blind, so we need to know whether your hotel is able to cater for his special needs. He has a guide dog that accompanies him wherever he goes. We hope that this will not be a problem for you or your staff.
  Your website says that you have "fully-equipped meeting rooms". Please could you explain what "fully-equipped" means and let us know how much it would cost to hire one of these rooms for half a day?
  We look forward to hearing from you.
  Best wishes,

Extra practice

Your own answers.

Get ready to write

Your own answers.
- *Your own answers.*
- *Your own answers.*
- *Your own answers.*

1 a 1 tells the reader about a holiday and ends with a reply to an invitation.
   2 starts off as a 'Thank-you' letter. The writer is thanking Fumiko for a birthday present. It also brings the reader up to date with news, and ends with an invitation.
   3 is a reply to the email in blue print from people who want to visit. It says the would-be visitors are welcome. It brings them up to date with family news.

b All the emails are between friends and update the reader with personal information about the writer and their friends or family. 1 and 3 are from one couple to another. 2 and 3 are between people of different nationalities. 1 and 3 are emails and are more informal than 2.

2 a 1 is a simple email.
      2 is a traditional letter.
      3 is the original email that was received with responses added.

   b 2 is the most formal while 1 is the most informal. 3 is more formal than 1 but more informal than 2.

   c Examples of informal language highlighted

1

> Hi Jon 'n' Jo
> Had a great time in Turkey – nice people, nice hotel, good food, perfect weather, interesting trips. Only real prob was flights – both delayed more than 2 hours. Got home last night at 1 o'clock. Glad you had a good time with Pete and Chris and others. Getting together – great idea but Tuesdays aren't good for us – how about Wednesday 21st?
> See you soon
> Cheers
> Matt and Tina
> BTW Hope you enjoy Libya.

3

3/4 *Your own answers.*

Focus on the language of informal emails

Rewritten extracts

1 Hi Matt
   Thanks for coming to the meeting yesterday. IMO – very useful. Sure you'll enjoy working with Debbie and John.
   I'll be in touch again soon.
   Cheers,
   Jenny

2 Juan,
   We got your letter this morning – thanks. Sorry you've been made redundant but glad you've got an interview next Wednesday. Let us know if you get the job. Good luck!
   Speak soon / Take care / Cheers
   Pieter

5 *Your own answer. Possible answer:*
   Dear Rosie,
   Congratulations! Great news about you and Sam. Thanks for the invitation – I'll definitely be there.
   I've had a pretty busy year. In January, Seb and I split up. It wasn't easy – we'd been together for nearly two years – we'd even been thinking about making it more permanent, but he met someone else. After that I couldn't work in the same office as him,

From: Silvia
To: Ed
Subject: Re: FW: Summer
Date: Thu, 15 Jun 2006 15:21:14

Hi Marco and Silvia,
I've been trying to email you but the mails keep bouncing back – probably an old email address. I hope this one gets through.
Hi Ed,
Good to hear from you! Sorry about our home email – clever idea to send it to Marco's work address! Marco's really busy, so he's forwarded it to me.
We're writing to tell you that we'll be staying at the campsite near you again this summer. First two weeks of August. This time we're flying, then hiring a car. Hope we can meet again.
Great news! Call us when you're here and we'll arrange a get-together. Perhaps we could go out for a meal – there's several good restaurants near here, like the pizzeria we went to last time. Remember?
Things are really busy here. Jackie's just started working as an assistant in a primary school and I have more freelance photographic work than I can cope with – suppose we shouldn't complain.
Know what you mean. I've just started a new job as a receptionist in a hotel just down the road – very handy, but I have to work weekends and evenings – so no holiday this year and big changes to family life!
Becky's just finished her first exams. In September she'll go to the local college (for 16–18-year-olds). Jo's just coming to the end of her third year at secondary school.
The boys have just started their summer holidays. Gianfranco just scraped through his exams! He'd much rather hang out with his mates. Adriano's done pretty well but he's got a different attitude to life. Both the boys've got scooters now. They seem to spend all their free time on them. The only good thing is, they're making less phone calls – they didn't used to go out at all.
Anyway, we hope you'll be at home when we're in Italy and that the weather's better than last time we met.
I'm sure we'll be around – just come round or give us a ring.

Best wishes to you all,

Ed and Jackie
Love
Silvia

so I applied for loads of jobs. I eventually got one as a doctor's receptionist. The money's not particularly good and the hours are long, but it makes a change – and I enjoy meeting people.

Do you remember my sister Ellie? Well, she's getting married next year, probably in August. And I saw Jack the other day. He asked about you. I hadn't had your letter then, so I couldn't tell him your news.

I've got two weeks' holiday coming up. The first week, I'm just going to chill out – catch up with friends, you know. Then I'm off to Crete with Jenny. I'm really looking forward to it. It'll be my first proper holiday for three years.

Anyway, congratulations again. Let's keep in touch more regularly. Why don't we email each other at least once a month?

Love,

Extra practice

Your own answer. Possible answer:

Hi Charlie,

Just had a message from Mum to say you're around for a week. That's great! Before you go back, let's get together. How about going for a meal at the new Turkish restaurant in town? I can do tonight or tomorrow?

You can phone my mobile (07818 417785) or email.

See you soon.

John

Unit3

Get ready to write

○ *Your own answers.*

◉ a   Place of birth / Maiden name: **Passport application form**
  b   Approximate value of item being claimed for: **Insurance claim form**
  c   Salary for the last financial year: **Tax return form**
  d   Briefly describe your injury: **Insurance claim form**
  e   Have you suffered from any of these health problems in the last 10 years?: **Application form for course / job / insurance / gym**
  f   Do you wish to transfer a balance from another card?: **Credit card application form**
  g   Academic qualifications: **Application form for course / job**

1 a   Extract 1 is a delayed departure claim form (section of travel insurance form). Extract 2 is a visa application form for the US.
   b   *Your own answers. Possible answers*:
      Extract 1 is probably preceded by basic personal information, e.g. name, date of birth, etc. It is probably followed by bank details so that insurance money awarded can be paid directly into claimant's account.
      Extract 2 is probably preceded by basic personal information, e.g. name, date of birth, etc. It is probably followed by more details of applicant's travel history, past visa applications (whether these have been successful or not), details of any criminal record, health records, etc.

2 a   Extract 1:
      –   The applicant has only given her first name (Natasha)
      –   Date of arrival is given as Beijing / Place of destination as 04/09/06

Extract 2:
   –   20 Full address of college in Paris not given
   –   22 Day and Month should also be given
   –   24 More details of address needed / Postcode needs to be added
   –   25 There are two phone numbers missing
   –   26 Applicant is very imprecise about how long he/she intends to stay
   –   27 Again this is too vague. Visa applications need to be more precise
  b   The form language in both extracts is factual, businesslike, concise and formal.
  c   In Extract 1 the language is factual, businesslike, concise and formal, and written in note form. In Extract 2, it is vague, imprecise and informal.

Focus on language appropriate to forms

1 a   Extract A is written in a more appropriate style because it is clear, formal and detailed. For example, it uses full forms, not contractions and uses formal words such as *approximately* rather than *about*. It also specifies that the other driver was on a minor road.
  b   Extract B is conversational – too informal for a report form like this. For example, it uses contractions instead of full forms, and uses informal words such as *about* rather than *approximately*. It misses out the important detail that the other driver was on a minor road.
  c   In an email or informal letter to a friend.

2 *Your own answer. Possible answer*:
   It was approximately 4pm when I left for the bank to withdraw some cash. I was out of my hotel room for no more than ten minutes. When I returned, I could see that someone had entered the room. My belongings were scattered all over the floor.

3/4 *Your own answers.*

5 *Your own answer. Possible answer*:

Personal Effects Claim Form

Section 2

Travel details

Type of travel: Business / Personal

Please give date of loss / theft _28 August 2006_
In which country did the loss / theft occur? _Italy (Milan)_

Please give full details of loss / theft   I arrived back at my hotel room at 10.30 in the evening to find the window open and my belongings on the floor. When I started to put things back in drawers and cupboards I found the articles listed below missing.

To whom was the loss / theft reported? _Hotel manager and Police_
When was the loss / theft reported? _Immediately (10.35pm) / 11.05pm_

What steps were taken to recover the articles? (Please attach any written evidence.)
   N/A – the articles were stolen, not lost.

Have you had any previous claims on this type of insurance? YES/NO
If YES, please give details, including dates.   N/A

Section 3

Particulars of claim

Full description of each item of property lost or stolen.	Date of purchase	Original price	Amount claimed	Receipts / replacement estimates attached
Laptop computer (Dell)	12/01/2004	€1200	€300	✓
Digital camera (Sony)	13/08/2006	€350	€800	✓
Gold watch (antique)	gift	€3000	€1000	not available
Glasses (Armani)	?/12/2000	€600	€300	✓

Section 4

DECLARATION

I declare that all the information given is to the best of my knowledge and belief, full, true and correct
Signed __Stefan Podolski__   Date: _17 October 2007_

Unit4

Get ready to write

○ *Your own answers.*

○ *Your own answers. Possible answers:*
The texts in List A are intended for an unknown general public readership whereas those in List B are to known individuals. The language in the texts in List B is likely to be more informal/casual, and may contain colloquial language.

1 a The subject of both letters is the introduction of ID cards.
 b The writer of letter 1 is against ID cards and feels they will not protect the public in the way they are supposed to and will provide a new incentive to criminals. He is also concerned about the high cost of introducing cards and feels that the government having access to personal information will be undemocratic. The writer of letter 2 is pro ID cards and feels they are a practical way of proving who you are. They are like a passport and increase freedom.

2 a 1 *they will put (not they'll) / I am quite sure / it is estimated*
  2 *I have carried / I am the owner / I did not have / I could not open*
 b 1 *I think that Mr Green is mistaken / I am quite sure that, like me, many of your readers*
 c 1 *it is estimated that the cost of the card system will be six billion pounds*
  2 *in Britain, people are required to provide household bills*
 d 1 *Far from putting an end to identity theft … whom Mr Green fears.*
 e 1 *… the conmen, hackers and would-be terrorists **whom** Mr Green fears.*
   *… the data bank **on which** my personal details will be stored?*
   (less formal equivalents in brackets)
   support (back) / *on the grounds that* (because) / *combat* (fight) / *mistaken* (wrong) / *ingenuity* (cleverness) / *incentive* (reason) / *citizens* (people) / *currently* (now) / *have access to* (be able to get at)
  2 *people are required to* (people have to)

3 Letter 1
 I think that …
 My strong personal belief is that …
 I genuinely believe that …
 I am quite sure that …
 In my view, …
 Letter 2
 It seems to me that …
 In my opinion, …
 I would say that …

Focus on qualifying opinion expressions

1 a firm/profound/genuine/honest/sincere
 b firmly/seriously/passionately/honestly/sincerely/really
 c (absolutely/pretty) certain
 d honest/personal/professional
 e general/fashionable/popular/traditional/official
2 a amazingly/surprisingly/unbelievably/incredibly
 b clearly/apparently/evidently
 c funnily enough / strangely (enough)

4 *Your own answers.*
5 *Your own answer. Possible answer:*
I am in complete agreement with Jenny Lavender (see Letters, Tuesday). In general, I believe that the majority of women are as well-equipped as men to fight on the front line in wartime. Although I have no direct experience of this myself, several members of my family, men and women, have spent time in the armed forces. With this in mind, I can honestly say that in some cases the women were better able to cope with the emotional pressures than the men. I have no reason to believe that this would be any different in a wartime situation.
The main reason for my point of view is this: women have been fighting for equality with men for decades now. In many countries, they have achieved equal pay with men for the same work. Their arguments have always been that the work they did demanded the same skills and abilities as their male colleagues. If we have been convinced by their arguments for equal pay for equal work, how can we possibly deny women the right to fight on the front line in times of war?
Secondly, and this may be a controversial point, I believe morale generally would be higher among armies if women were allowed to fight on the front line. In this situation, which is stressful for everyone concerned, it seems to me that a "normal" mix of men and women could only raise morale.
In conclusion, I believe, as does Jenny Lavender, that the arguments against women becoming front-line fighters are based on old-fashioned sexist attitudes. Men may want to protect us from the horrors of war, but we need to prove that we are strong enough to fight alongside men.

Unit5

Get ready to write

○ *Your own answers.*
○ *Your own answers.*
○ *Your own answers.*

1 Letter 1: repair/servicing
 Letter 2: products from a shop
 Letter 3: accommodation
2 1 c 2 b 3 e 4 f 5 d 6 a
3 Paragraph 1 introduces the topic of the complaint
 Paragraph 2 provides more details/background to the complaint
 Paragraph 3 suggests how the problem can be resolved
 Paragraph 4 is a final expression of what the writer expects

Answer key

4 a *resolve this unsatisfactory situation*   b *seeking advice*
c *contact me*   d *I purchased*   e *(is not) fit for purpose*
f *speedy (1); swift (2)*   g *You are required by law to*
h *amicably*   i *maintenance of the property*
j *the deteriorating condition*

5 *Your own answers.*

Focus on avoiding repetition

2 *Your own answers. Possible answers:*
   a I should be grateful if you could contact me
      Please get in touch with me
   b I look forward to hearing from you
      I am looking forward to receiving your reply
   c I shall be forced to / I will have to
      I shall have no option but to
      My only option will be to
   d I am writing to let you know / inform you
      This is to inform you
   e I am writing to confirm

6 *Your own answer. Possible answer:*
   Dear Sir,
   On 23 April I was due to attend an important meeting in Chicago.
   I had a seat on the 12.15 flight from Heathwick Airport.
   To make sure I did not miss my flight, I decided to catch the 07.45
   train from my local station. Unfortunately, the train did not arrive
   until 08.45 and was further delayed due to a 'staff shortage'. We
   did not leave the station until 10.45. Needless to say, I missed my
   flight to Chicago. I explained the situation to the airline staff, but
   still had to buy another ticket. I arrived in Chicago considerably out
   of pocket and very late for my meeting.
   I am now writing to complain about this appalling rail service and
   to demand a full refund, not only of my rail fare but also of my
   replacement air ticket. Please find attached details of these costs.
   I look forward to hearing from you. I should be grateful if you
   would contact me at the above address or by phone.
   Yours faithfully,

Extra practice

Your own answers. Possible answers:
a I am writing to inform you that it is your responsibility to solve
   this problem, and if you do not do this, I shall have no choice
   but to contact my solicitor.
b I am not satisfied with this situation. You promised to return my
   call on the same day, but you failed to do this.
c This is a most unsatisfactory situation and I now wish to know
   how you intend to resolve the problem.
d As you may remember, I telephoned you two months ago on
   the subject of the television I had recently purchased from you.
e I should be grateful if you would refund my payment in full. If
   you do not do this, I shall be forced to take legal action.
f I have now written two letters to you during the last fortnight. I
   should be very grateful if you could reply.
g If I do not hear from you in the near future, I shall have no
   option but to contact the police.
h I would expect a company of your reputation to replace the
   fridge by the weekend at the very latest.

Review 1

1 Answers and mistakes are shown in red below.

Customer complaints department
Follow-up form

Date 15 July 2007

Customer details
Name Mr / Mrs / (Ms)   ~~Elena~~   Helen   O'Brien
Address ~~17,~~ 27 The Avenue, , EN16 4HM N
Phone number 01707 ~~888173~~ 888163
Bank account number 22 76 93 54

Details of the complaint
1 Date of transaction or poor service
   Day 16   **Month** May   **Year** 2007
2 Date of first complaint?
   Day 16   **Month** June   **Year** 2007
3 Contacts spoken to previously at bank
   Customer doesn't know

Brief summary of your complaint
On 16 ~~April~~ May customer phoned to cancel a direct debit to electricity
company.

On 15 June customer noticed that this regular payment to the
electricity company had left her account as usual.

Customer phoned the bank and was told that cancellation would be
actioned.

But money taken from account again in July.

Action taken
Report to General Manager. Recommend full refund + compensation
payment to customer.

Someone should phone customer ~~tomorrow.~~ later today

---

2 a E b E c B d B e E f E
3 a by the way   b for your information   c in my opinion
4 a I'm b I c I d Have you e I'm
5 *Your own answer. Possible answer:*
   Hi,
   Thanks for your letter – it was great to hear from you after such a
   long time and find out what you've been doing since we were last
   in touch.
   I'm sorry I can't reply properly at the moment – I'm revising for
   my exams which start on Monday.
   As soon as the exams are over, I'll write you a long newsy letter
   telling you what I've been up to.
   Cheers,
6 *Your own answer. Possible answer:*
   I will soon be receiving my exam results, which I am confident
   will be good; perhaps not the top grades, but certainly very
   acceptable. After that, I am not sure what I will be doing. I would
   like to work for your company on a temporary basis, but this is
   dependent on my situation in two months' time.

Answer key

7 *Your own answers. Possible answers:*
a firm/profound/genuine/honest/sincere
b firmly/seriously/passionately/honestly/sincerely/really
c absolutely/pretty

8 a 1 to 2 which 3 had 4 than 5 not 6 if
7 throughout/during 8 has 9 it 10 without
b *Your own answers.*

9 a 4 b 5 c 1 d 6 e 7 f 3 g 2

10 *Your own answer. Possible answer:*
On 16 December, my suitcase went missing from flight 4536 Berlin to London Heathrow. I reported this in person to one of your ground crew on the day in question and followed this up with a telephone call three days later. To date, I have had no response to my phone call.

Unit 6

Get ready to write

- People usually write CVs when applying for a job or other position of responsibility. The CV itself contains mainly factual information about the person, but may also include a brief commentary on this information if the writer wants to present a clear, full picture of themselves.
- All these categories have a place in a normal CV with the exception of *Family background* and *Likes and dislikes in music, food, etc.*, which would be considered too personal and therefore irrelevant.
- From an employer's point of view the following extra information might be useful:
Address(es) / Contact details (Phone, email, etc.) / Date of birth / Nationality / Gender
In some situations, it is not necessary for job applicants to state their age or gender, as this could prejudice their chances of success.

1 The writer has probably chosen to start with her academic achievements because she has only recently left university and it is therefore more relevant than her work experience.

2 a Approximately a quarter of the CV consists of commentary.
– *I have run classes at a local adult education centre.*
– *I enjoy travelling to other countries and meeting people from different cultural backgrounds. I have travelled widely in SE Asia, and Europe.*
b This commentary is in 'normal' written sentences with subjects, verbs, objects, etc. It is clearly written in the first person. This is unlike the impersonal, note-form language of the rest of the CV.

3 *DOB*: date of birth
BA: Bachelor of Arts (This is the name of one of the first degrees in British universities). Other "bachelor" degrees are BSc (Bachelor of Science), and BEd (Bachelor of Education).
Econ: Economics
Hons: Honours degree (Degrees from British universities are divided into Honours and Ordinary degrees. With Honours degrees there are classes: a First / a 2.1 / a 2.2 / a Third)
Adv.: Advanced
IELTS: International English Language Testing System – Students who wish to study at British universities often need a certain score in IELTS in order to get on to an undergraduate course.
SE (Asia): South East
Dr: Doctor

4 A covering letter adds a personal touch that the factual information in a CV does not. It tells the reader something about what you are like as a person, and gives them an idea of whether or not you would make a suitable employee.

5/6 *Your own answers.*

Focus on reducing full sentences to notes

a Driving test: passed 2007
b English fluent – written German good
c Prize for A grade in Business Management project
d BA (Hons) Economics from London University, 2006
e Member of working group (2006 report: 'Staff–management communication issues')
f Assistant to Head of Human Resources, Oct 2005–Jan 2007

7 a *Your own answers.*
b *Your own answer. See model on page 33.*
c Covering letter
Dear Australian Tours,
I am writing in response to your recent advertisement regarding the post of Tour Guide. Please find enclosed my CV which summarizes my education, qualifications, skills and experience.

I have been looking for a job like the one described in your advertisement for some time now, as I believe I have the skills and experience needed for this kind of work. I did a similar job during a vacation from university two years ago. My employers were very satisfied with the work I did and would be happy to provide me with a reference.

I am currently employed as an instructor in an outdoor pursuits centre for young people and this work has given me experience of dealing with groups of people, and of working irregular hours. I am used to being away from home for periods of up to a month. Part of this job is to take groups of 10-15 people on weekend trips to remote parts of the country; one of my responsibilities is to organize the cooking. I also deal with any injuries or health problems that arise while groups are away, and have a First Aid Diploma.

In relation to the other qualifications needed for the Tour Guide job, I have been driving now for nearly five years and have a clean licence. As regards my level of English, I am bilingual in English and Italian.

I would be available to come for interview at any time, and look forward to hearing from you.

Yours faithfully,

Unit 7

Get ready to write

- A written recommendation by a present employer to a possible future employer describing an employee's character, skills and qualifications.
- *Your own answer. Possible answer:*
a Job references are necessary information or evidence for a future employer from someone who knows an applicant well, either as a friend, colleague, or employer.
b–c *Your own answers.*

1 Differences between the two extracts:

Extract 1	Extract 2
1 In continuous prose, like a letter	1 Note form
2 No headings to guide the writer	2 Notes under headings as guidelines
3 Reference writer decides priorities	3 Headings dictate priorities

2 b 1

Examples:

I have known and worked with (full verb forms)

he is someone for whom I have the greatest respect (word order)

contributed greatly (choice of vocabulary)

Notable among these projects (fronting information)

c 2

Examples:

(He) *Has shown leadership skills* (omission of subject pronoun)

Excellent, both as (a) *team leader and* (a) *team member* (omission of articles)

d *Your own answer.*

e *Your own answer.*

Focus on formal language in relative clauses

1 b Notable among these projects was his setting up and management of Project Peru, <u>the success of (which) was largely due to Ben's commitment and leadership skills.</u>

c Reading the description of the job <u>for (which) he has applied,</u> I can honestly …

2 b Notable among these projects was his setting up and management of Project Peru <u>whose success</u> was largely due to Ben's commitment and leadership skills.

c Reading the description of the job <u>(which/that) he has applied for,</u> I can honestly …

3 b My colleague Juan is someone with whom I have always worked very well.

c That is a question to which there is not a single answer.

---

3 a *Your own answers.*

b *Your own answers. Possible answers.*

1 The person's current job, course or situation

2 How you know the person / How long you have known him/her

3 General character and attitude to work

4 Relationships with other people (colleagues/students)

5 Past successes and achievements

6 The person's particular skills and abilities

4 *Your own answers. See model on page 37.*

Unit 8

Get ready to write

◯ *Your own answers. Possible answers:*

a A transport service: train, bus, airline   b A supermarket or other large store   c Car/Flat rental company   d Airport/Airline   e Employment agency / Job centre / Unemployment benefits office

◯ *Possible additional questions*

a Are you generally very satisfied, satisfied or dissatisfied with the efficiency of our drivers and other staff?

b Parking at the store is adequate.
Agree __ Not sure __ Disagree __

c Were you given clear instructions about returning the vehicle at the end of the rental period?

d Did you find the standard of service from our staff …
Above expectations, Met expectations or Below expectations in the following areas …

e What is your current weekly wage?
– less than £200 ☐
– £200–£250 ☐
– £250–£300 ☐
– £300–£400 ☐
– more than £400 ☐

1 a Airline passengers in ten European countries.

b Fly-U-There came first out of 70 airlines for quality.

c Lower fares for the minority who would accept a lower standard of service in exchange for a reduction in standards. More leg room for the passengers who found the seating 'cramped'.

2 a Order of headings:

Punctuality / Assistance with problems

Quality in relation to price

Staff–passenger relations

In-flight comfort / Catering

b They clearly signpost the information contained and help readers find relevant information.

3 The first two paragraphs introduce the subject of the report and summarize the main findings.

4 b took part   c judged   d were analysed   e was given   f scored

---

Focus on reduced relative clauses

1 Parts of sentences which could be expanded into relative clauses <u>underlined</u>, with the addition of relative pronouns and auxiliary verbs (in bold):

– According to a recent customer satisfaction survey, **which was** <u>carried out by an independent market research organization,</u> …

– Customers, **who were** <u>interviewed during a flight,</u> seemed more satisfied than those who returned written questionnaires

– Customers, **who were** <u>asked for their views on relations with staff,</u> commented favourably on the friendliness, …

2 *Your own answers. Possible answers:*

a <u>Most people questioned</u> said they were very happy with the service.

b <u>The questions, chosen at random,</u> focused mainly on people's experiences over the last four weeks.

c <u>The results produced by the survey</u> show that only a small minority are seriously dissatisfied.

d <u>The service, introduced last year,</u> faced serious problems in its early stages.

5 a *Your own answers. Possible answers*:

    2   22% of customers agreed that the store was 'well laid out'.

    3   A very large majority of customers thought there was an insufficient number of checkouts.

    4   69% of customers did not think that the shop was well laid-out

    5   Only 5% of customers were not sure whether there was a sufficient number of checkouts.

    6   Equal numbers of customers agreed and disagreed with the statement that the store was 'clean and tidy'.

  b The two areas where customers were most satisfied were 'clear and informative signs' and 'a pleasant shopping atmosphere'.

  c The two areas where customers were least satisfied were 'shop layout' and 'number of checkouts'.

6 *Your own answer. Possible answer (reduced relative clauses are shown in bold type and verbs from Exercise 4 are underlined)*:

Supermarket: Customer report

According to a recent survey **carried out by one of the country's three largest supermarkets**, customers were dissatisfied in three main areas: store layout, ease of moving around the store, and the number of checkouts. 4,500 customers <u>took part</u> in the survey.

Checkouts

The area of greatest dissatisfaction was the number of checkouts. 86% of customers thought there were not enough, with only 9% satisfied in this area.

Store layout

Over two thirds of customers questioned agreed that the store was well laid out. A similar proportion said that the store was not easy to move about in. Perhaps surprisingly, a majority of customers said they found the signs in the store clear and informative.

Cleanliness

Equal numbers of customers agreed and disagreed with the statement that the store was clean and tidy.

Atmosphere

This was an area where the supermarket <u>scored</u> highly, with 61% of customers <u>judging</u> that the store had a 'pleasant shopping atmosphere'. This is good news for the supermarket managers, who will interpret this as meaning that most of their customers enjoy shopping in their stores.

After <u>analysing</u> the survey results, the manager of the supermarket in question has said they are planning to make some key improvements in the near future. He said their priority was to ensure that more checkouts were open for longer. He also promised to look again at the layout of the store.

Extra practice 1

Your own answers. Possible answers:

a … expect to work until the age of 70 at least.

b … efficient staff to clear labelling.

c … there will be increases in transport fares this year.

d … there were areas where improvements could be made.

e … is planning to reduce the tax on basics like food and power.

Unit 9

Get ready to write

○ *Your own answers.*

○ *Your own answers. Possible answers*:

  A How much does it cost? Does it work with all phones:

  B Could it ever suggest the wrong route? Does it work in other countries?

  C How much does it weigh? Is it possible that it could collapse while you are riding it?

  D Would it be sensible to get insurance in case you had an accident? Are you allowed to use them in normal pedestrian areas?

1 Powerizers – We know this because the advertisement on page 44 says that Powerizers allow you to run fast and jump high, which both appear in the notes under 'Key features'.

2 a detailed notes about the product

  b a note-taking framework

  c recommendations for action

3 a Basic b Competitive use c ✗ d ✗ e 30 f 2

  g sports h exercise / keeping fit i children under 12

  j elbow pads k helmet

4–7 *Your own answers. See model on page 45.*

Focus on noun phrases

1 b two-cup model

    c fully programmable model d heatproof handle

    e deluxe self-cleaning model

2 a three-year guarantee b everlasting, ultra-efficient bulb

    c water-powered battery d 2GB memory stick

    e camping survival kit

Unit 10

Get ready to write

○ *Your own answers.*

○ *Your own answers.*

1 a 2

  b *Your own answers. Possible answers*:

    Words, phrases or sentences that could be omitted from the other three are underlined. [Note: some of these omissions would involve rewriting of remaining words and phrases.]

  email 1

  Dave,

  Thanks for looking at the figures – <u>you're quite right</u>, those two small amounts were errors – <u>entirely my fault</u>. <u>From the end of this month</u> we are launching a <u>large new</u> e-commerce store <u>at the site</u> that automates the calculation of sales information and payments – <u>so the manual aspect will be entirely removed.</u>

  <u>We've grown really quickly and the new store software will take us to the next level – look out for an announcement during this month.</u>

  Cheers

  Joe

email 3

Dear Conference Member,

<u>Renate has asked me to email you to</u> check that you will not be attending the evening meal on Thursday 17 May. This is because you have elected to leave the conference before 8.00 pm on that day.

<u>We apologize for the fact that the times of meals may not have been made clear in our original conference invitation.</u>

Regards,

Melanie Dean

email 4

Joe,

Please send the electronic report again. It's not opening on my compter <u>for some reason.</u>

Thanks.

Chris

<u>PS Have a good holiday if I don't see you before.</u>

2 – beginnings and endings: *Dear* is not always used with names. Simple endings are often used, e.g. *Cheers* and *Regards* instead of the more formal *Yours sincerely* or *Yours faithfully*.

– the structure of the email: These four emails look like short, very simple letters.

– sentence construction and length: Sentences are mainly simple (i.e. without subordinate clauses etc.).

– the degree of formality: Emails are often neutral in terms of style – neither very formal, nor very informal. They tend to be direct, rather than extremely polite.

3 *Your own answers.*

4 *Your own answer. Possible answer:*

Notes
- Kate – email Ed   • Late – here 12 o'clock
- Flexitime meeting – for everyone not just parents with young children – limit on start and end times: 7 am – 8 pm (not during night)
- Kate's sorry

5 *Your own answers. Possible answers:*

Reply to email:

Nick,

Re meeting: okay Thursday pm and all Friday. Thoughts on agenda:

1 Not complete ban – restrict use

2 North? Property cheaper

3 Yes – with limit

Nothing to add.

Cheers

Email related to phone conversation:

Ed,

Kate phoned. She's going to be late. Had thoughts about flexitime:

– Can't restrict to parents of young childr. Must be open to all.

– Suggest start and end times – 7 am – 8 pm (not during night)

K said sorry.

Regards

Focus on short simple sentences

Your own answers. Possible answers:

a Apologies for the payment delay. The system couldn't process your invoice. Coding errors.

b Please transfer all our savings from our Gold Account to the Direct Savings Account.

c Please return the grant application form sent on 10 November. To have your application considered for the next academic year we need the form by the end of this week. Please send to the address above.

Extra practice 1

Your own answer. Possible answer:

Jeremy

Re our telephone conversation of this morning, I now wish to confirm the order of a new office photocopier – model OC850/C2 (colour).

Please let us know approx. delivery date ASAP.

Regards,

Extra practice 2

Dear Renate,

Unfortunately, the working lunch we had provisionally planned for 21 August has had to be cancelled. We are now proposing the following alternative dates: 27 August, 3 September, 12 September. On each date the meeting would begin at 9.30 am.

I would be very grateful if you could let me know as soon as possible which of the above dates you are available on, and which of the three you would prefer. I hope to confirm one of the dates by the coming weekend, or by Monday at the latest.

Apologies for any inconvenience.

Best wishes,

Unit 11

Get ready to write

○ *Your own answers.*

○ b Practise c keep d Make e Sell f Start g Show h Refer i Mention j Write k include l list m explain n gained o say p attend(ing)

○ *Your own answers.*

1 a teach in a primary school

b a first degree (BA in Philosophy)

c Citizenship, History and English

2 a In general the writer has followed the tips quite well, but improvements could be made.

b An improved order of paragraphs would be: 4, 1, 3, 5, 2.

c The last part of paragraph three (from *There is many other factors ...*) is relatively trivial and could therefore be omitted.

d There is no evidence in the statement that the applicant has researched the particular course she is applying for in any detail, even though she makes a general statement about the reputation of the Edinburgh course.

e The style of this statement is sufficiently formal, although the many mistakes spoil what otherwise could have been a good impression.

3 Grammar error / Spelling error

The correct forms are given in [square brackets].

I have a variety of experience of working with young people in both academic and non-academic situations. Throughout my undergraduate course, I undertaken [undertook / have undertaken] voluntary work at the local infant school. I found this very enjoyable and rewarding, as I often helped groups of less able children with specific tasks and found it very satisfing [satisfying] to see them begin to make progress.

In addition to my academic study, I have a number of interests. I play tennis, and badmington [badminton] to a reasonable club level and have recently taken up rock climbing. I also love reading and going to the theatre.

When I was working on a summer play scheme, I took responsibility for a larger group of children aged 8 to 12 for a whole day, thoroughly enjoying the experience. I also recently acompanied [accompanied] a group of Year Six pupils from Milan on a week-long English-language coarse [course] in Scotland. Both these experiences influensed [influenced] my decision to specialize for [in] Upper Primary teaching. I felt I could really stimulate and communicate with this age group and found the feedback I recieved [received] from the children very rewarding. There is [There are] many other factors which could be useful in my future career. I was captain of my school tennis team between the ages of 10 and 12; my mother and father are both teachers here in Italy, and I was always very interested in watching any TV programmes about teaching and education.

In selecting the Postgraduate Certificate in Education at edinburgh [Edinburgh], I am making a concious [conscious] choice of a course which will challenge and test me to the full. Your course has a formidable reputation in the training of primary school teachers. My first degree course, which was a BA in Philosophy, was largely text-based and involved writing regular essays, thus utilizing my written, language, research and analytical skills. The emphasis on moral, social and political issues have [has – the verb is singular here because the subject of the verb is *emphasis*] increased my awareness of a variety of contemporary debates, thereby equipping me to tackle themes relavant [relevant] to the classroom, such as social skills and equal opportunities. The content of my course will assist me in contributing to a wide range of school curriculum areas, in particular Citizenship, History and English, all of which are backed up by my own school-level qualifications.

Focus on writing complex sentences

1 Complex sentences in Carla Pacione's statement:
   - **When** [conjunction] I was working on a summer play scheme, I took responsibility for a larger group of children aged 8 to 12 for a whole day, thoroughly **enjoying** … [participle] the experience.
   - **In selecting** [participle clause] the Postgraduate Certificate in Education at Edinburgh, I am making a conscious choice of a course **which** [relative pronoun] will challenge and test me to the full.
   - My first degree course, **which** [relative pronoun] was a BA in Philosophy, was largely text-based and involved writing regular essays, thus **utilizing** [participle clause] my written, language, research and analytical skills.
   - The emphasis on moral, social and political issues has increased my awareness of a variety of contemporary debates, thereby **equipping** [participle clause] me to tackle themes relevant to the classroom, such as social skills and equal opportunities.
   - The content of my course will assist me in contributing to a wide range of school curriculum areas, in particular Citizenship, History and English, all of **which** [relative pronoun] are backed up by my own school-level qualifications.

2 *Your own answers. Possible answers*:
   a I think I am well suited to a career in law because I enjoy studying social issues in today's society, and believe that I have the skill to use factual evidence to present a persuasive argument.
   b I think my contributions to class discussions have improved, probably due to the fact that I have developed my knowledge of the subject, which has in turn made me more confident about speaking in front of the whole class.
   c My personal experience of journalism started when, as a young child, my father took me with him when he went to interview people for articles he wrote for a magazine.

4–6 *Your own answers.*

7 *Your own answer.* *See model on page 53.*

Extra practice

Your own answers. Possible answers (changes shown in bold):
I first became interested **in** composition, **which** is now my **musical** passion, **while** I was working for my 16+ school exams. This passion is reflected in my ambitions, **which** include composing for films, television and radio. In addition to my studies I **spend** a **considerable** amount of my free time **composing**. **By studying** English and Music Technology **as well as** Music at school, I hope to help another of my ambitions, **which** is to **write** a musical.

Answer key

Unit 12

1 You know that the rest of the talk will focus on the six remaining factors affecting people's happiness. ('In my talk I shall be considering eight of the factors which may or may not affect people's happiness.')

2 a Symbols – ∴, +, →
Abbreviations – *v.*, *N .B.*
Capital letters – *HAPPINESS, MONEY, CAN, BUT, DESIRE, LESS, LIMIT*
Shortened words – *hap., Mon., Comp., imp. peop.*

b *Your own answer.*

c You might choose to add notes on the fact that happiness levels have remained the same despite the fact that people's income has increased dramatically. Example:
Incr. in income ≠ incr. in happiness.

3 *Your own answers. Possible answer:*
I would have used bullet points. I could have used other symbols such as = .

4 *Your own answer.*

5 *Your own answer. Possible answer:*

> HAPPINESS – Factors 3 – 5
>
> 3 _____ and hap.
>
> 4 _____ and hap.
>
> 5 _____ and hap.

6 *Your own answer. Possible answer:*

> HAPPINESS – FACTORS 3–5
>
> 3 INTELLIGENCE and hap.? – NO connection
> · More intelligent peop. better-paid jobs ∴ richer BUT not happier
> · Poss. have higher expects. ∴ less satisfied
>
> 4 Genes and hap.
> Hap. 90% genetic
> But personality + hap. connected, e.g. extroverts happier
>
> 5 Appearance and hap.
> Good-looking people happier
> WHY?
> · good-look. better lives?
> · good-look. = symmetric. faces = good genes & health
> Advice: Believe you look good.

9 *Your own answer. Possible answer:*

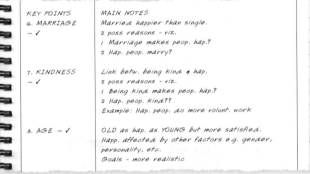

KEY POINTS	MAIN NOTES
6. MARRIAGE – ✓	Married happier than single. 2 poss reasons - viz. 1 Marriage makes peop. hap.? 2 Hap. peop. marry?
7. KINDNESS – ✓	Link betw. being kind 4 hap. 2 poss reasons - viz. 1 Being kind makes peop. hap.? 2 Hap. peop. kind?? Example: Hap. peop. do more volunt. work
8. AGE – ✓	OLD as hap. as YOUNG but more satisfied. Happ. affected by other factors e.g. gender, personality, etc. Goals - more realistic

Focus on selecting and noting key words, and paraphrasing

1 *Your own answers. Possible answers:*
~~In a~~ study of 2727 people ~~aged between~~ 25–74, ~~researchers found that other things such as~~ gender, personality type and social factors affect how you feel as you get older. ~~For instance, both~~ men and women ~~tended to experience~~ more positive emotions ~~as they aged~~.

2 *Your own answers. Possible answers:*
– study of 2,727 peop. (25–74 yrs.)
– gender, personality type & social factors affect how you feel as peop. >> older
– Men + women have more positive emotions

3 *Your own answers. Possible answers:*
– 2,727 25–74-yr-olds studied
– Various factors influence feelings as people age
– Men + women feel more positive

Unit 13

- a 1 b 3 c 2
- *Your own answers.*
- *Your own answers.*

1 *Your own answers.*

2 Card 1: Introduction to subject
Card 2: Two examples
Card 3: Public reactions to commercials
Card 4: Advertisers' motivation
Card 5: Conclusions

3 *Your own answers. Possible answers*:
a Capital letters are used for headings/titles of cards.
b Highlighting is used for key words or ideas under each heading.
c Bullet points are used to separate points on each card.
d Words used – mainly nouns, adjectives, some verbs (these words all carry meaning.)
Words not used – articles and other determiners (e.g. this), possessive adjectives, conjunctions, some prepositions (these are words which do not carry meaning.)

4 *Your own answers.*

5 *Your own answers. Possible answers*:
- Both cards and handout follow the same order as the spoken presentation
- Handout is closer to the presentation than cards in terms of detail
- Cards are more skeletal and therefore need interpretation, explanation or commentary
- Handout should be detailed enough to stand on its own as a reminder of the content of the presentation
- Cards intended to help the speaker who has prepared the presentation
- Handout intended for people who have listened to the presentation

Focus on omitting unnecessary words

Possible answer:

A television commercial, often called an advert in the UK, is a form of advertising in which goods, services, organizations, and ideas are promoted via the medium of television. Most commercials are produced by an advertising agency, and airtime is purchased from a TV channel or network.

6–13 *Your own answers.*

Extra practice 1

Your own answer. Possible answer:
CHANGE IN COMMUNICATION HABITS: YOUNG PEOPLE
- Past – telephone: landline and mobile
- Now – text messaging: 100+ texts per day
b *Your own answer. Possible answer*:

1 Change in communication habits among young people
1.1 Increase in text messaging
1.2 Change from telephone (landline and mobile) to text messaging.
1.3 Some young people send and receive 100+ texts a day.

Unit 14

- a short account of something spoken or written which gives the important points but not the details
- Types of summary
  - News headlines are a very condensed version of the fuller story which follows.
  - The blurb on the back cover of a paperback novel tells the potential reader what the book is about, but is not a full summary because it does not tell the whole story or the ending.
  - A newspaper account of a scientific report gives the main findings of a report that would be too long or complex for a non-specialist reader.
  - Most diary entries are very brief summaries of something that is going to happen or has happened.
  - Students' notes summarize a lecture, BUT use note form language rather than normal prose.
  - A radio report of a sporting even summarizes by providing the highlights of the game/match.
The other texts would not be summaries.

- *Your own answers.*

1 The best title is 2 'Mummies' DNA reveals origins of ancient disease' because it contains all the key aspects of the story. 'Archaeologists discover disease in ancient DNA' does not relate the ancient disease to the present day situation, while 'Leishmaniasis originates in North Africa' makes no mention of the role of DNA or mummies in establishing the origin of the disease.

2 *Your own answer. Possible answer*:
[Centuries of silence cannot keep ancient Egyptian mummies from sharing their secrets with scientists. From archaeologists determining cultural practices to chemists studying embalming, mummies have revealed libraries of information.] Now such mummies are also yielding evidence about the diseases of the past by giving up the facts encoded in their preserved DNA, and new research may have established the ancient origin of a modern disease.

Leishmaniasis — [a disease caused by microscopic parasites, like malaria, and transmitted by sand flies – results in painful skin sores and in its most vicious form] causes at least 500,000 deaths worldwide every year. Today it affects communities in many parts of the world The lethal form – [visceral leishmaniasis, also known black fever] – is particularly prevalent in North Africa.

Albert Zink [of Ludwig-Maximilians University in Munich and his colleagues] tested the DNA of bone samples from 91 ancient Egyptian mummies and 70 from old Nubia – modern Sudan — to determine if they had suffered from leishmaniasis. In 9 of the 70 Nubian mummies, taken from graves stretching as far back as A.D. 550, DNA of the parasite was discovered, proving the disease was endemic at least that far back. It is highly probable that it has even more ancient origins; four of the Egyptian mummies carried the parasite's DNA, each dating from the Middle Kingdom period of 2050 to 1650 B.C., when trade ties with Nubia were strongest. Egyptian mummies from prior and later periods showed no sign of the disease.

Answer key

[In addition to highlighting the old cultural ties between Egypt and Nubia, it also] adds further weight to the theory that visceral leishmaniasis first developed in Nubia. And the technique has been applied to other diseases, [such as tuberculosis and malaria,] to trace their development. 'We can contribute to a better understanding of the evolution of infectious diseases and, thereby, to a more efficient treatment and control of those diseases,' Zink says. The infections and viruses that proved a curse to ancient mummies may yet provide a cure for ancient scourges that still plague humanity.

3 *Your own answers.*

4

Original	Summary
a evidence about the diseases of the past	information about past diseases
b 500,000 deaths worldwide every year	500,000 deaths annually
c The lethal form … is particularly prevalent in North Africa	The deadly type … is found mainly in North Africa.
d trade ties with Nubia were strongest	strong trade links with Nubia

---

Focus on *this, that, they, them* and *it*

1 a the researchers   b 2050 BC and 550AD
   c the research into leishmaniasis   d other diseases

2 *Your own answers. Possible answers*:
   a Malaria is an infectious disease, common in tropical and subtropical parts of the world. <u>This disease / It</u> is spread by female mosquitoes.
   b Malaria infects between 300 and 500 million people every year, and causes up to three million deaths. Most of <u>these deaths</u> occur among young children.
   c Experts claim malaria is a huge public health problem. <u>They</u> say <u>it</u> is a cause of poverty.

---

5 *Your own answer. Possible answer*:

Jurassic "beaver" is largest early mammal yet

A new fossil from China proves that the mammals that lived during the Jurassic era were more diverse than previously thought. The 164-million-year-old creature, known as Castorocauda lutrasimilis, had a tail like a beaver, the paddling limbs of an otter, seal-like teeth and probably webbed feet. [And although most Jurassic mammals discovered thus far were tiny, shrew-like animals, C. lutrasimilis would have weighed approximately a pound. Roughly the size of a small, female platypus,] it is the largest mammal from this time period on record.

Chinese archaeologists [led by Qiang Ji of Nanjing University] found the well-preserved fossil, [including impressions of soft tissue and fur], in Inner Mongolia. [Other fossils had hinted that mammals might not just have been small terrestrial creatures until the demise of the dinosaurs] 65 million years ago, but the beaver-tailed animal definitively pushes back the date of mammalian adaptation to an aquatic lifestyle by at least 100 million years. ['Based on its relatively large size, swimming body structure, and anterior molars specialized for [fish] feeding,] Castorocauda was a semiaquatic carnivore, similar to the modern river otter,' [the team writes in the paper announcing the find in today's issue of *Science*.]

The discovery also highlights how little is known about early mammals. [Most are represented by teeth and jaws alone. 'We stand at the threshold of a dramatic change in the picture of mammalian evolutionary history,' argues mammalogist Thomas Martin of the Senckenberg Institute in Frankfurt, Germany in an accompanying commentary.] 'The potential of fossil-rich deposits in Liaoning Province in China or in Inner Mongolia is only just beginning to be exploited.'

6 *Your own answer. Possible answer*:
   – New fossil found in China shows that a range of mammals existed during the Jurassic era
   – The mammal is called Castorocauda lutrasimilis
   – Similar to a beaver, a seal and an otter
   – The largest mammal recorded from this time
   – Chinese archaeologists found the fossil which shows that mammals adapted to living in water 100 million years before it had been thought
   – Castorocauda lutrasimilis was carnivorous water mammal, similar to an otter
   – This shows how little we know about early mammals
   – Experts expect more discoveries to be made in areas of China and Mongolia rich in fossils

7–8 *Your own answers.*

9 *Your own answer. Possible answer*:
A new 164-million-year-old fossil found in China shows that a range of mammals existed in the Jurassic era. Castorocauda lutrasimilis, which was a carnivorous water mammal similar to a beaver, a seal and an otter, is the largest recorded mammal from this time period.
Chinese archaeologists found the fossil which shows that mammals adapted to living in water 100 million years earlier than had been thought previously. The discovery proves how little we know about early mammals, but experts expect more revealing discoveries to be made in fossil-rich areas of China and Mongolia. [93 words]

Extra practice 1

Your own answer. Possible answer:
A 164-million-year-old fossil found in China shows that a range of mammals existed in the Jurassic era. Castorocauda lutrasimilis, a carnivorous water mammal similar to present-day water creatures, is the largest recorded mammal from this time period.
Chinese archaeologists found the fossil, which shows that mammals adapted to living in water 100 million years earlier than had been thought. The discovery proves how little we know about early mammals, but experts expect to make more discoveries in China and Mongolia. [80 words]

Extra practice 2

American crayfish are making European crayfish extinct. Males are attracted by natural female chemicals and scientists use this to attract crayfish, then remove them from rivers.
This will control crayfish which have escaped into UK waterways.
The largest crayfish from a British river weighed 200g.

Unit 15

Get ready to write

○ *Your own answers.*

○ *arguments for and against an idea* and *the writer's opinions* are common features of discursive essays. *Facts and figures* may be included if they support an argument or point of view.

○ Best order for essay-writing steps:
1 Work out what the essay question means and think about your own views on the question.
2 Check exactly what you have to do and how much to write.
3 Write a paragraph-by-paragraph plan for your essay.
4 Find information on the subject, for example from a library or the Internet.
5 Organize relevant information and your ideas on the subject.
6 Write a first draft.
7 Check your language, spelling, punctuation and style, then correct if necessary.
8 Write your final essay.

1 *Your own answers.*
2 Title B
3 *Your own answer. Possible answer:*
People become stressed because they cannot achieve the right balance between the pressures of work and their family commitments.
4 a Overwork can lead to relationships being neglected 3
  People agree that stress is on the increase and understand the reasons 1
  The importance of a balanced lifestyle 4
  People need to be financially secure 2
  Time management is the key 5
  b 1 I will start by examining
    2 I would say that / In my opinion / It is a commonly held view that
    3 (tensions) may arise / this can cause (stress)
    4 In conclusion
    5 for instance
  c The style of writing is formal. For example, the writer uses full forms rather than contractions (*I will* rather than *I'll*) and uses formal rather than informal words and expressions (*occupation* rather than *job*, *are unable to* rather than *can't*).
5 The topic under discussion is climate change. Two points of view are mentioned: firstly, that something must be done immediately to prevent a global catastrophe on the Earth, and secondly, that climate change is the result of natural processes, not human activity. *Your own answers.*

Focus on punctuation – the use of commas

1

Use of commas	Examples from sample
– between items on a list	– *on people by their jobs, family commitments, financial worries and other pressures* – *money to feed, clothe and provide accommodation*
– after a subordinate clause at the beginning of a sentence:	– *If they have no time to relax with their children, tensions may arise between family members*
– before and after words or phrases which interrupt the flow of a sentence	– *Families, however, need more than financial security* – *In my country, for instance, many people live in*
– After adverb phrases at the beginning of a sentence	– *In my opinion, they do this by managing their time* – *In conclusion, I would say that people*
– Before (or before and after) a non-defining relative clause.	– *accept anti-social working conditions, which may include night working, or take on …*

2 a All along the route, we could see beautiful wooded gorges, shimmering lakes, silvery rivers and majestic waterfalls.
  b The Windy Islands, which are north of Sicily, are fantastic. If you are near enough, stop there for a while.
  c Suddenly, out of the blue, one of three boys walking towards me rushed up to me, shouted something I couldn't hear and grabbed my bag, in which I had all my valuables: my wallet, my mobile phone, my camera and my return train ticket.
  d From what I have seen of the documentaries, some of the most beautiful shapes and colours of the world are found in plants, fish and other organisms that live on the seabed.

7 *Your own answer. Possible answer:*
There can be no doubt that human activity poses serious threats to the environment. Obvious examples are our misuse of energy and our accelerating consumption of natural resources. The former is contributing to global warming, while the latter is causing serious waste disposal problems. Whoever we blame for this damage, one thing is certain: everyone suffers from its effects. Unfortunately, the most serious problems, such as global warming, are so enormous that they are beyond the capability of individuals to solve. In such cases, governments and international organizations should take a lead, by, for example, agreeing to limit greenhouse gas emissions. It is their responsibility to pass laws to control the situation in their countries. Taxpayers' money should be used to fund large-scale projects, and businesses and individuals should be fined if they break environmental laws. Once governments have established policies, it is the responsibility of each individual to translate those policies into action in their lives. In addition to this, however, there are actions that only individuals can take. For example, only individuals can decide whether to use public transport instead of driving their car; and only individuals can sort household waste, plastics, paper, glass and metals into

separate bins for collection. In our apartment block, for instance, although the majority of residents sort their rubbish in an environmentally friendly way, a few do not.

In conclusion, I would suggest that the answer to the question, 'Whose responsibility is it to look after our planet?', is simple. Our planet will only be protected effectively if governments and individuals work together.

Extra practice 2

a The Everglades stretch for hundreds of swampy miles across Southern Florida, home to hordes of snakes, alligators, and assorted creepy-crawlies, but now an invasion by deadly giant pythons is threatening the eco-system of the famous partk.

b The pythons, which are thought to have been released into the wild by careless pet owners, are no ordinary snakes. They are Burmese pythons native to South Asia which can grow 6 metres long, weigh 100kg and live for 20 years or more.

The pythons have established breeding pairs in the swamps and are racing to the top of the food chain, even getting rid of alligators, which were previously the top predator in the Everglades.

'It is a very serious issue, especially as we have found breeding pairs and clutches of eggs. That means they've adapted to living here and they are having a big impact,' said Linda Friar, an official at Everglades National Park. The snakes are a serious threat to indigenous wildlife due to their big appetites and expansive tastes.

Unit 16

Get ready to write

○ Picture A is a bar chart. Picture B is a line graph. Picture C is a pie chart.

○ *Your own answers.*

○ *Your own answers.*

1 a Red = the figure for 2000; Blue = the figure for 2005
  b In most countries unemployment rose in the period 2000–2005.
  c In Bulgaria, unemployment fell from over 16% in 2000 to 10% in 2005.

2 a Denmark had the highest employment rate, while Poland had the lowest employment rate.
  b *Your own answers. Possible answers*:
    Malta had almost ten percent fewer people in employment than Luxembourg.
    The Netherlands had a significantly higher rate of employment than Belgium.

3 a The report takes longer to read and analyse, but it can offer explanation and analysis of the findings, whereas the table and bar chart can only give information.
  b 1 *increase, rise slightly, fall (slightly), down, up*
    2 *broadly*
  c *slightly, broadly*

4 a the telephone
  b the mobile phone
  c ownership of consumer durables increased steadily

Focus on ways of referring to statistical trends and movements

2 g 3 f 4 c 5 b 6 d 7 a

6 *Your own answers. Possible answers*:
  With one exception, the ownership of consumer durables in the UK rose significantly from 1998–99 to 2004–05.
  To start with the exception, ownership of telephones fell slightly in this time period from 95% in 1998–99 to 92% in 2004–05. There was a trend in the opposite direction in the case of mobile phones, where ownership rose dramatically from around 27% in 1998–99 to 79% in 2004–05.
  The proportion of households owning a home computer rose from 33% to 62% during this period. The percentage of households with an internet connection also rose sharply, from 9% in 1998–99 to 53% in 2004–05.
  In the area of kitchen-based consumer goods, the percentage of households with access to a dishwasher, a tumble dryer and a microwave rose to 33%, 58% and 90% respectively in 2004–05. This compared with 24%, 51% and 79% in 1998–99.
  Overall, it is clear from the figures that ownership of almost all consumer durables increased steadily in the five year period in question.

Extra practice

Your own answers. Possible answers:

– From 2000 to 2004, the total number of people in work in the 15-19 age group fell from 8.3 million to just over 7 million.

– In comparison, in the same period, those in the 20-24 age group who were employed rose from 14.3 million just over 15 million.

– In both years and in both age groups more men than women were employed.

– In 2000, just over 7 million women between the ages of 20 and 24 were employed, compared with 6.7 million in 2004.

Review 2

1 a IELTS b BA c DOB d Hons e Dr f Econ

2 a Extensive experience of business management (practices)
  b Long-term aim: to set up own company
  c Gained honours (1st) in biology
  d Recent work: developing new computer software
  e Ambition: manage major company by age 30
  f Regularly attended courses on Business Management
  g Organize holidays for children with special needs in spare time

3 *Your own answers. See model on page 32.*

4 a 4 b 6 c 1 d 5 e 2 f 3

5 *Your own answer. Possible answer*:
  As manager of the marketing department of the company, I have known Mr Suzuki for over five years. For the last two years, he has worked closely with me on the reorganization of the department. Mr Suzuki has a thorough understanding of good business practices and works quietly but efficiently to reach his targets. He remains calm and good-natured at all times. His main achievement at our company has been to introduce major changes in working practices without alienating colleagues. He is an excellent manager of people and popular both with those above and below him in our organization.

6 a The people to whom I am writing are all ex-colleagues.

b The employee for whom I am writing this reference has worked for the company for over ten years.

c The projects in which he has been involved have all been successful.

d The colleagues with whom he has worked here all speak very highly of him.

7 a The compuer I'm working on is absolutely state of the art.

b Brad Ellis is the manager we're responsible to.

c Gerry is someone I've got the greatest respect for.

d The meeting you're referring to took place on 17 June.

8 *Your own answer. Possible answer*:

On the question of passenger comfort on our buses, the report shows that a large majority of our customers were satisfied or very satisfied. Only 34% were not satisfied.

When we asked about the punctuality of our bus services, only a small number of passengers (16%) were very satisfied but almost two thirds were satisfied. This left only a fifth of passengers who were not satisfied.

On the question of driver politeness, a total of 95% of passengers questioned said they were very satisfied (65%) or satisfied (30%). This left a very small minority of five percent who were not satisfied.

When we asked about the cleanliness of the vehicles, only 25% were very satisfied, with 40% satisfied, and the remainder (35%) not satisfied.

Finally, on the question of driving quality, 70% of passengers were very satisfied, with 20% satisfied and only 10% not satisfied.

9 *Your own answer. Possible answer*:

Item	Bike–U–Fold fold–up bicycle
Models	• Men's
	• Women's
Suitable for	• Bicycle riders aged 12 and over
Plus points	1 Environmentally friendly
	2 Light and easy to carry
	3 Takes 10 seconds to fold up and unfold
Price	• $99

10 a Members of the public invited to take part in the survey were all sent a personal letter of thanks written by the Head of Research.

b The survey forms, completed online, were analyzed by a group of sociologists specially trained for the purpose.

c The results published in the newspapers represent just a small proportion of the data collected in the survey.

11 a I am organizing an 18th birthday party at the Octane Club on 30 April next year. I am looking for a band.

b Would you be available to play for this event? How much would you charge for playing 8.00 – midnight?

12 a I am very/particularly interested in following this course because I have always enjoyed learning languages.

b I was awarded 'A' grades for German and French and a 'C' for Russian. I have also travelled to / visited all three countries for holidays, and therefore/consequently have frequently practised speaking.

c We also have satellite TV at home, which can receive foreign channels, so I try to watch French, German and Russian programmes whenever I can.

d I also have penfriends in all three countries, and attempt to use their languages. However their English is excellent, so we write in English on most occasions.

13 *Your own answer. See model on page 32.*

14 *Your own answer. Possible answer*:

SAVING = key to financial success.

–everyone needs PLAN …

• to meet long-term goals

• financial security

PLAN (BUDGET) creates money to save

Steps

1 set short- and long-term goals (e.g. new car)

2 say how long & how much money

15

> Researchers ~~from three universities~~ interviewed 20,000 people ~~over a~~ 2-year period ~~to produce the~~ most in-depth study to date ~~of this kind~~. Most ~~of the~~ findings ~~were what researchers had~~ predicted, but attitudes towards ~~the~~ future ~~were~~ surprising. ~~Of the~~ 5,000 people under ~~the age of~~ 30, ~~a large~~ majority (79%) ~~said they were generally~~ pessimistic about the future. ~~Of those over the age of~~ 60, 70% ~~said they felt~~ optimistic or very optimistic ~~about the future~~.

Your own answer. Possible answer:

Notes

In depth-study:

– 20,000 people interviewed in 2 years.

Findings: Mostly predictable, BUT attitudes to future surprising:

– 5000 under 30s – 79% pessimistic.

– Over 60s – 70% (very) optimistic

16 *Your own answer. Possible answer*:

1 At birth

Babies born with basic sensory capacities e.g. vision/hearing

Babies can distinguish between visual forms but get bored

Look again if a new visual stimulus is presented

2 After a few days

Babies recognize mother's face and voice. Proof: look/listen longer

3 Evidence that babies recognize mother's voice at birth, from womb?

4 Babies need continual stimulation in early years for sensory systems to develop

17 *Your own answers. Possible answers*:

1 Babies at birth have vision and hearing.

2 Few days later, recognize mother's face / voice

Also at birth? From womb?

3 Babies need stimulation for successful development

18 The question 'Why do we use language?' seems hardly to require an answer. But, as is often the way with linguistic questions, our everyday familiarity with speech and writing can make it difficult to appreciate the complexity of the skills we have learned. This is particularly so when we try to define the range of functions to which language can be put.

'To communicate our ideas' is the usual answer to the question – and indeed, this must surely be the most widely recognized function of language. Whenever we tell people about ourselves or our circumstances, we are using language in order to exchange facts and opinions. This is the kind of language that will be found in reference books – and in any spoken or written interaction where people wish to learn from each other. But it would be wrong to think of it as the only way in which we use language. Language scholars have identified several other functions where the communication of ideas is an irrelevant consideration. Such functions include 'emotional expression' and 'social interaction'.

Your own answer. Possible answer:
The answer most people give to the question 'Why do we use language' is 'to communicate our ideas' but language use is more complex than this. Most speech and writing may involve exchanging facts and opinions, but language has other functions, where the communication of ideas is irrelevant. These include expressing emotions and social interaction.

19 a Many birds migrate, but the Arctic tern travels furthest. It flies from the Arctic to the Antarctic, then back again, which makes a round trip of 32,000 kilometres.

  b Some animals can regrow parts of their bodies if damaged. For example, the starfish, which has five arms, can grow new ones. Another such example is the slowworm, which can regrow a broken-off tail, something which lizards can also do.

  c The giant squid, whose eyes can be 39cm across, has the largest eyes of any animal. This is 16 times wider than a human eye.

20 b, c and f

21 a In my opinion, digital technology is making the world a safer, more pleasant place to live.

  b During his long working life, my grandfather was a policeman, a farmer, a gardener and a lorry driver.

  c Anost, which is in the Morran district of France, has a music festival every year.

  d Apples, bananas and oranges are quite sweet. Lemons, by contrast, are sour.

  e Although there's a speed limit of 60kph on this road, many drivers go over 100kph.

22 *Your own answers. Possible answers*:

  a Opening paragraph:
  The millions of motorists who use the roads every day would probably agree that there are too many private cars on our public roads. Some people believe that many of these motorists should be using alternative forms of transport. Year by year the need to solve this problem becomes more and more urgent. One of the solutions that has been suggested is to charge motorists for every mile they drive.

  Closing paragraph:
  In conclusion, I would say that motorists who use the most crowded public roads at peak times should be charged quite steeply. This will encourage motorists to drive at other times or to leave their cars at home and travel by train or bus instead.

  b Opening paragraph:
  In many countries children leave school between the ages of 16 and 18. Some continue their education at university or in other forms of higher education. There is a proportion of children, however, who take no interest in school work and are just waiting for they time when they can leave. Some people argue that these bored, restless children should be allowed to leave school early and start work.

  Closing paragraph:
  In conclusion, I would say that the best way to deal with bored, restless children is not to simply let them abandon their education at the age of 14, but to provide them with a more relevant, meaningful or enjoyable educational experience.

23 *Your own answers. Possible answers*:

  a 322 million English speakers use the Internet. This is nearly 30% of all users.

  b It is estimated that a total of 1.340 billion people are Chinese speakers, but only 144 million of these are internet users.

  c 7.9% of internet users are Japanese speakers. This represents 86 million out of a total of 128 million people in the world who speak Japanese.

  d A similar percentage (7.5%) of internet users speak Spanish, although it is estimated that 437 million people worldwide are Spanish speakers.

  e Out of a total number of 98 million German speakers, 58 million are internet users. German speakers make up 5.4% of internet users.